Word From the Top

The Chief Executive's Guide to Business Communication

By

Thomas E. Fuszard

© 2001, 2002 by Thomas E. Fuszard. All rights reserved.

No part of this book may be reproduced, stored in a retrieval system, or transmitted by any means, electronic, mechanical, photocopying, recording, or otherwise, without written permission from the author.

ISBN: 0-7596-8260-7

This book is printed on acid free paper.

1stBooks - rev. 03/15/02

Excerpts from *The Wall Street Journal* are used with the permission of the publisher, Dow Jones & Company, Inc.

Certain products and services mentioned in this book are properties of other companies: PowerPoint is a registered trademark of Microsoft Corporation; Netscape is a registered trademark of Netscape Communications Corporation; and Freelance is a registered trademark of Adobe Systems, Inc.

Acknowledgments

I am indebted to numerous friends and associates for their patient reviews, generous comments and great encouragement in the preparation of this book. I am especially grateful to my special friend Laurie Hurley; to author and half-century pal Dave Schaefer; and to trusty longtime partner Tom McDonnell.

Many thanks to mentors and friends Bob Blair, Jim Connell, Dean Miller, Mike Ervin, Sandra Bell, Ron Kirkpatrick, Don Kirk, Ron Johnson and Ken Pilone.

Thanks also to Lisa Campbell and Mary Dreyer for their thoughtful editing.

Remembering Harold and Margaret Fuszard,
to whom all books were great treasures

Table Of Contents

Page

The Written Word 1

Why we write • What we write • What it says about us • Polishing your writing skills • Writing for the ear • Vocabulary • Knowing when to stop • Page fright • Writing to one reader • Getting to the point • Writing around barriers • Humor • Editing • Vague language • Roundabouts • Focus on the reader • Humility • Writing positively • Short sentences, short words • Outlining • When to write • Reviewers • Sources • Staying fresh • e-Mail • The annual report • Managing writers

The Spoken Word 43

Types of presentations • Stage fright • How to make them care • Previewing the group • Two-minute drill • Rehearsal vs. practice • The audience • The messages • Reasonable expectations • Preparation • Getting attention • Set the schedule • Brevity! • Powerful organization • Sharing the outline, materials • How to start, stop • Humor • Enumerate • Solicit response • Say it, write it • Say it with pictures • Get moving! •

"Bridge words" • The recap • Q&A • Graphic aids • The details • The script • About your voice

The Word in Meetings..87

Common complaints • Time-management arithmetic • Why meet? • Other methods • Invitation lists • Agendas • Meeting leadership • The site • Equipment and materials • Timing • Disharmony • Q&A • Recap • Follow-ups • Ending fearlessly

The Heard Word..97

Importance of listening • Developing listening skills • Passive/active listening • Establishing rapport • Recognizing biases • Timing • Hidden messages • Body language • Hold your tongue! • Outline imaging • Note-taking • Learn to ask/ask to learn • Confirmation

The Last Word...109

Preface

Business leaders come from a remarkable variety of backgrounds—corporate finance, manufacturing, engineering, logistics, the law, occasionally medicine and the other sciences. But extremely rare is the chief executive officer whose primary training is in communications, such as the leader of an advertising agency or another communications-related business. For the most part, chief executives have come to the job with little formal training in writing and speaking.

Nevertheless, the chief executive is expected to be the voice of the corporation—the executive who not only establishes and carries out policy and strategy, but articulates it as well. Shareholders, securities analysts, lawyers, lenders and legions of employees may hang on this individual's every word.

In forty years in the business community, I've had occasion to observe many chief executives and their communications styles. A few chief executives are gifted communicators. Most are pretty good. A few are hopeless.

This book is for the "most." It is intended not as a text in remedial writing or Speech 101, but as a guide that offers some tips on improving the creation and delivery of messages "from the top." It deals with several communications topics: business writing, particularly in the form of letters, memoranda, plans and reports; speechwriting and vocal presentation skills; and meetings management. A section on listening skills is included as a kind of appendix to which I hope you'll turn when you find yourself speaking more and listening less.

T.E.F.

Word From the Top
The Chief Executive's Guide to Business Communication

The Written Word

Introduction

Why do we write?

Two reasons, mainly. We write to commit ideas to a movable medium and to make the ideas available later, when the originator is not at hand.

You try to call Tom to exchange information about a project, but find that he's on vacation for two weeks. As he returns, you're leaving for two weeks, so you'll not be in communication by telephone for at least a month. Had you reached him, you and Tom would have exchanged information about the project, made suggestions and perhaps agreed on who is to do what. Both of you would have been required to remember most of what was said.

But since you missed connections, you had to commit your ideas to writing. Now, think about what Tom can do with your message when he returns from his holiday: read it, re-read it, circulate it, edit, ask for comments, take it home—all kinds of things he could not do with information from the phone call, had it been connected. Your words will be as fresh in two weeks, and in a month, as they are the day you wrote them. Likewise the words of William Shakespeare, as alive today as at the turn of the 17th Century.

Thomas E. Fuszard

What we write

How do we use this wonderful skill in business? A half-dozen ways.

To inform or report: *I wish to advise you that those wonderful sales results I promised have failed to materialize.*

To persuade: *Just give me one more chance to drive your new car, and this time I won't crash.*

To request action: *You should act right away; the sale ends today.*

To correct or clarify: *The booklet you were sent in Swedish may have failed to inform you. Here is a copy in English.*

To express appreciation: *Thank you very much for sending me your brother-in-law's resume.*

To apologize: *We sincerely regret the misconduct of our sales representative at your company's Christmas party.*

What we're saying

How well or poorly we communicate these six kinds of messages says volumes about us and about our organizations to people we may never meet. Society tells us that good, clear writing reflects good, clear thinking. We are thought to be smart, articulate, well educated and cultured. The reciprocal is equally true; poor writing, careless punctuation and sloppy spelling say a lot about us.

I picture a person of my generation, perhaps a marketing man with 35 years under him. He writes regularly to the field—letters, memos, sales bulletins, reports, go-get-'em stuff. He's been in the job for so long, he's widely known by dealers, distributors and customers, but only through his writings. What he <u>thinks</u> they're thinking is: *They love this stuff. They think I'm really terrific.*

But based on what they know of him from his writings, what most people out there <u>are</u> thinking is: *I wonder how this guy finds his way to the men's room.*

Message: The care expressed in your writing makes a huge difference in the way you and your company are regarded.

Polishing your writing skills

It's easy. It is fast, simple, comfortable and effective. Best, it doesn't require that you go back to your freshman year in high school to review grammar. Besides, your grammatical style was set long ago, and nobody is likely to change it at this point in your life.

Most executives—indeed, most business writers—don't lack the ability to write; they lack *confidence* in their ability to write. So, this is about helping you to find more confidence. It's about helping you to strike out with a bold pen.

We are told that a fifth of all working Americans are functionally illiterate, as defined by their inability to comprehend the written instructions needed to change a tire. My guess is that 90 percent of the remainder don't write at all, simply because their work doesn't require it. The airline captain who brought you to where you are, the flight attendant who brought your lunch, the person who built your office, and in fact most of the people in your company probably write very little.

That leaves a relative handful of us—people in the business community whose work requires that we write something sometime. A letter, a memo, a plan, a report.

For many of us, this is a disagreeable task. I liken it to the person who's pushing a shopping cart through the supermarket and finds that it has a sticking wheel. The more you put into the cart, the worse the wheel sticks. And it stays that way all through the store, until you reach the checkout counter.

Grocery shopping is supposed to be relatively pleasant, or at least pain-neutral, so you find this sticking wheel a particular annoyance. You tell yourself, "It isn't supposed to be this difficult."

That's my metaphor for the writing job, as seen by many business people. We'll break our pencils, erase repeatedly, beat up our word processors, all in frustration about some simple writing task. And we say, "It isn't supposed to be this difficult."

It isn't. Let me offer some tips, suggestions and ways to get along with business writing more rapidly, effectively and comfortably.

Faster, better, easier, right?

How to Make it Better

Ask two questions

Originate all your business communications in the two questions:

- Who are you trying to reach? and,
- What do you want them to do?

Think about it: just about everything you need to write aims to get others to do something—buy a product, lend some money, understand a problem, pitch in and help, maybe just go away.

But we don't start that way. We start by thinking about others' reactions to our message, and we tend to worry that the reader or readers are better able to use the language than we are. Most of them are not, of course, so you're worrying needlessly.

The message: Keep the mission in mind as you write. You'll find this makes your writing shorter and more pointed.

Remember, too, that you're not here to create something pretty; you're here to move a business message.

Write for the ear

Most of us have been hearing the English language for a long time, so our ears are tuned to discern the difference between correct and incorrect grammar. This is a neat kind of "filter" that helps us to edit our work. I recommend reading aloud anything of more than a sentence or two; if a subject and verb don't agree, for example, you're more likely to hear it than see it.

Remember, too, that we write mainly to record speech. So, if your writing sounds like your usual speaking style, it's done right.

Let you be you, and write as you speak.

Thomas E. Fuszard

Stop worrying about your vocabulary

The largest compendium of the English language contains more than 600,000 entries. An unabridged American dictionary might contain a quarter-million. Of these, we use a relative handful: 25,000 or so for an adequate business vocabulary; 30,000 a good one; 50,000 at the top.

Moreover, of the words within the grasp of our understanding, we use precious few. Experts say we use fewer than 50 words to communicate half of what we say and write, and a tiny handful to communicate one-fourth. (They don't make a good sentence, but for memorability I sort the most popular words into a phrase that sounds vaguely Shakespearean: "*...and have you the will to be of it?*")

If you are concerned about your ability to communicate, and if you blame what you think is an inadequate vocabulary, you're putting the blame in the wrong place. Perhaps you need to consider other ways to say the same things, so as not to sound trite or repetitious. A vocabulary built from a few thousand short, lively, tough, simple, Anglo-Saxon words will help you communicate substantially everything you need to say.

Know when to stop

The most serious shortcoming in executive writing is not that the writer doesn't know how to start, but that he or she doesn't know how to stop. Most corporate prose is overwritten, overexplained, overdone.

So, tell the reader what the reader needs to know; then stop.

If you begin a letter by reminding your readers, "As I indicated in my letter of November 28th...", you will chase them back to the files to find it. Refer to something outside your message *only* if it is essential that it be recovered and referred to in connection with the current communication. For that matter, if it's essential, you might attach a copy.

If you still can't decide where to stop, try the end of the first page. Rarely must a letter or memo be longer than that. Remember that the Gettysburg Address has fewer than 300 words and the Ten Commandments, which help guide the ethical and moral conduct of more than a billion people, contain only about 75. If what you have to say is more important than those, go ahead and use a second page.

Page Fright

It's about confidence

An executive says, *"I'm not a bad writer...I'm a deliberate writer."* Another: *"I'm not bad at this stuff, but it's slow."* And another: *"I'm a pretty good writer, but it's torture for me."* One is heard to say, *"I can't see you Tuesday; I have to spend the afternoon writing a memo."*

I hear these comments as, *"I'm intimidated by the blank page."*

I call that *page fright*.

Why are we afraid to write? Several reasons. We're afraid to be wrong, to be embarrassed, to appear poorly educated. Society, after all, equates speaking and writing ability with education, sophistication and culture.

Another reason is that we're afraid the piece we write will live forever. And here we're onto something. Companies throw away nothing, especially since a PC or terminal appeared on every desk. Unlike file cabinets that show their clutter, computer files are hidden away, so nobody seems to mind that we save every scrap of information.

Thus we fear that what we've written will surface someday to embarrass us—not an unreasonable fear in this litigious society. The answer: If you don't want it to embarrass you, don't put it in writing.

Still another reason we're afraid is that most executives practice their vocal skills more than their writing. The chief executive, in particular, says what's on his or her mind by telephone, in meetings, in videoconferences and in face-to-face conversations. Few are trained in the writing craft, so it's understandable that few would be comfortable with it.

Dealing With Page Fright

A few suggestions can help you write faster, better and more comfortably. At least some of them work for everyone by improving confidence and controlling page fright.

Enumerate points when you can.
Most of what you need to write has in it more than one problem, more than one solution, option, idea, product, place, model, whatever. If you start by making the list, you'll find that your message needs little more than an introduction and a conclusion.

I need to write to Frank, who's been working on a project for a long time. I must explain to him why I voted against its continuation in yesterday's meeting.

So, I explain that I voted to discontinue the project for five reasons:

1. the product's burdensome weight;
2. its high production cost;
3. the shipping distances involved;
4. the outlook for gross margins; and
5. our shortage of trained technicians.

My message needs a gentle lead-in and a concluding line, and it's finished.

Numbered or bulleted items are simple to write and edit, since they often involve incomplete sentences requiring little skill. They're easy to comprehend and remember, too.

In your next written communication, try to isolate the three ideas, four suggestions, twelve models or nine places visited and put them into a numbered or bulleted list. You'll be amazed to see how little needs to be added, and how short and punchy your message becomes.

Write to one reader.

As chief executive, you often have occasion to write to the entire workforce. If that's more than a handful of people, it can be difficult to convey your meaning with feeling. That can be especially important if you're writing about downsizing or other disruptions in the employees' lives.

Don't try to write to all 12,000 people. Write to just one. Pick one you know who's likely to be interested and involved in what you have to say. If you begin with "Dear Ellie," you will tend to write with more feeling than the usual employee messages that sound like bulletin-board postings.

When you're finished, change "Dear Ellie" to "My Fellow Employees" or some other usual greeting.

Try to make it an editing job.

Much as we like to feel that we're trailblazing pioneers in the business environment, most of what we have to say has been said before. Take a look back at the way you described this situation the last time, or the way your predecessor dealt with it.

You'll have one of two reactions:

> *This is nonsense; I can do much better.*
> - or -
> *There are good ideas here, and I can use lots of them.*

Either way, you're not working from the blank piece of paper that we all find so intimidating.

Outline it.

Your fourth-grade teacher taught you to do this, and like most of us you probably haven't done it for years. Writing while you stare at the wall above your word processor, or at the clutter on your desk, means you'll have to change a lot of things around later that could be organized right from the start. It's much easier to write from a dozen words on the back of an envelope than from a blank sheet on a legal pad.

Put down the dozen words and change and rearrange them until they make sense. Then, write. And don't let anything stop you. The real work of writing is in the editing, not in creating that scratch draft. Write it to the end and put it aside for a while. Overnight is about right.

Get to the point.

In most cases, I'd start with the bottom line.

> *Here is the information you asked for...*
> *Sales in the second quarter topped our forecast by...*
> *I regret that we cannot honor your claim for...*
> *Three factors contributed to our third-quarter earnings decline...*

You will be amazed by the brevity of your messages when you deliver the news up front. And you'll be surprised by the confidence you will feel in explaining the situation after you blurt out the news in the first line.

Somebody figured out that American businesspeople are interrupted on average more than a half-dozen times an hour. The phone rings, an e-mail signal fires off, somebody stops by, the mail arrives...

If this is true, your reader will have trouble getting through a page-long letter or memo to get to the real news. That's another reason for putting the news up front.

One possible exception: bad news. Sometimes it's necessary to draw a word picture for the reader before delivering unpleasant information.

Write around barriers.

English teachers hate to hear this, but the plain fact is that you don't have a huge library or a house grammarian at hand, so sometimes it's necessary to avoid troublesome or puzzling constructions.

You've written *the town I grew up in...* and you know it's not grammatically correct. You know that *the town in which I grew up* probably is better, but it's not you. So start over, using any of dozens of other ways to say the same thing: *where I grew up...in my home town...back home...in Boise, we used to...*

I've heard carpenters urging one another along in the framing of houses, saying, "Come on—we ain't buildin' no piano." Remember that you're not building a piano here, either; just trying to move a simple business message.

So, don't waste a lot of time searching for the best possible grammatical construction. Chances are, you won't find it, or it won't suit your usual communication style. Go for the next-best—the one that's comfortable for you.

Make it your own.

Put your fingerprints on the piece you're writing. Try something different—something that will put a little personality into it. You'll be surprised at the confidence this lends.

A client chided me for writing that a company's results were aided by a *superb harvest* of a certain commodity. He said, "Tom, a really good harvest wouldn't be superb—it would bountiful."

Well, okay. But my choice of *superb* was purposeful, as I wanted to say <u>anything but</u> bountiful.

Think about the many ways one can say that a building is on a good foundation: *firm, solid, sturdy, strong, rugged.* We've heard them all, right? *Firm foundation, solid foundation.* But what if the architect says, "*I've put this building on a hearty foundation!*" Is that wrong?

Heck, no. He's being expressive, and what he's said is a lot more memorable than the too-familiar *firm foundation.*

Use some humor.

Very carefully, please. Using a slightly humorous twist in certain writings can take the sharp edge off a sensitive message. That said, please remember that there are more ways to be wrong than right in using humor.

I sat next to a man I knew slightly on a Los Angeles-New York flight. He talked on and on about his company, then asked what I did for a living.

When I explained that I'm a communications consultant, he offered to send me a packet of his company's materials to see if they needed help. We exchanged cards, shook hands, promised to be in touch and parted company in New York.

Then, nothing. Here I was with a perfectly good business prospect who seemed to have forgotten our conversation. I wrote this:

Dear David:

I haven't received your annual and quarterly reports or proxy statements. You aren't waiting for my check, are you?

Sincerely,

That's not the funniest line ever written, but it served to remind my prospect in an inoffensive way. He sent the material and apologized for having forgotten.

Another CEO asked me to edit an annual report that he said "missed the mark." Time was very short, and I couldn't get to it right away but wanted him to give me another couple of days. My e-mail message began, *Edit your annual report? I'd kill for the chance.*

The chief appreciated my eagerness and gave me the time I needed.

Some cautions are in order. We Americans love to tease, and we often forget that teasing humor can be cutting. Sometimes our desire to be funny outruns our good judgment. So, turn the teasing on yourself if you use it at all—perhaps calling attention to your own imperfections. Self-effacing humor goes down well in this society, and it's hard to make a serious mistake with it.

I can tell you it's humbling to come home after leading your company to a record year and finding that you don't know how to put together a kid's Christmas bicycle.

- or -

Life seemed so much simpler when I was one of the company's green-pea sales reps—young, eager, brash—yes, and dumb.

- or -

How do I feel about the kind of year we had? Well, if you've ever hit your thumb with a hammer...

The "nevers" include anything to do with race, religion, ethnicity, gender, sexual preferences, handicaps, politics...

You know the rules.

Edit savagely.

My last point about controlling page fright is the best advice I can offer. Nothing will improve your writing more than aggressive editing.

In Strunk and White's *The Elements of Style*, which contains more wisdom about writing than books with many times its fourscore pages, William Strunk, Jr., says:

Vigorous writing is concise. A sentence should contain no unnecessary words, a paragraph no unnecessary sentences, for the same reason that a drawing should have no unnecessary lines and a machine no unnecessary parts. This requires not that the writer make all his sentences short, or that he avoid all detail and treat his subjects only in outline, but that every word tell.

Co-author E. B. White, adds, "There you have a short, valuable essay on the nature and beauty of brevity—sixty-three words that could change the world."[1]

Most of us can spot in a minute a piece of business writing that hasn't been edited. It's lengthy, disorganized, rambling and stuffed with redundancies and useless jargon. It's usually written in a passive voice and has the main message at the end.

Start by throwing away a third of everything you write. Trust me, your work will survive. And trust me, it will be much better. Three pages become two, three paragraphs are two, and there are no page-and-a-half letters or memos. If you don't think you can make those kinds of cuts, go back to a quick re-reading of the Gettysburg Address; maybe also the Ten Commandments.

Think about cooking, and about what happens when you turn up the heat under a pot containing three quarts of sauce. When the three quarts have boiled down to two quarts, you find that the sauce is thicker and richer. It smells better. It tastes better. It's a better product. So is our language, after we cook out some of the nonsense.

---

[1] William Strunk, Jr., and E.B. White, *The Elements of Style*. Needham Heights, MA: Allyn & Bacon, 1979.

Magic happens when you edit aggressively, and it doesn't require that you remember any rules:

- Useless jargon goes away;
- Redundancies disappear; and
- Active voice replaces passive language.

Peel away useless language.

You've written *at this point in time,* or *at this particular point in time.* Now you're editing, and this discipline gives you a budget of just one word. Any problem converting it to *now*?

How about *in the event that,* which easily becomes *if?*

Or, something a little more corporate: *We made the strategic decision to close the Yakima plant as a cost-control measure.* How about, *We closed the Yakima plant to reduce costs.*

(*Strategic,* incidentally, is badly overdone in American business, where it seems every decision has become a strategic one. I'm expecting to read that some corporate staff made the strategic decision to go to lunch.)

Pursuant to your request, we have prepared, copied and enclosed a set of instructions for this device easily becomes *Here are the instructions you requested.*

In order to initiate action with respect to your refund, it will be necessary to ask you to advise us of the name of the merchant from whom you purchased the product. That's horrid. Try, *Please let us know where you bought it so we can process your refund quickly.*

Trashing the useless language makes your message not just shorter, but a lot better.

Kill redundancies.

The second benefit of aggressive editing is that redundancies go away. I enjoy highlighting redundancies because they're sort of silly, and because we're all guilty.

Ever talk about a *warning* without calling it an *advance warning*? How about *general consensus* or *consensus of opinion* instead of *consensus*, which of course means general agreement or concord.

Most of us talk about our *past history* and *future plans*. We say *new product introductions, free gifts, general public, acute crisis, totally destroyed, temporary reprieve, future potential, joined together, successfully rescued, foreign imports, few in number* and *commute to and from*. There are many more, of course.

Redundancies are like junk food in our language. Like useless words, they're squeezed out under the pressure of aggressive editing. *Past history* becomes *history, future plans* become *plans, advance warnings* become *warnings, commute to and from* becomes *commute*. It's another improvement in your written work, also without the need to remember any rules.

Find the active voice.

The third kind of improvement that occurs under vigorous editing is the shift from passive voice to active voice. You've written *reach a conclusion* and edit it to *conclude*. You change *made the assumption* to *assumed* and you replace *in a dominant position* with *dominates*.

Your writing takes on new vigor. It's shorter, more pointed, more effective—all without remembering any rules.

Caution: if you change *every* passive construction to active voice, you may end up sounding like a drill sergeant. Remember that the ear sometimes needs relief from the hammering of always-active voice. Give it a break now and again.

You might use the passive voice to soften a comment: *You would be advised to remove your child from the gallery.* Or, it can be used when you intend to be vague: *The decision has been made to downsize your department's staff.*

The Declaration of Independence employed both active and passive voice as it stirred patriot sentiment against George III. Active: *He has plundered our seas, ravaged our Coasts, burnt our towns, and destroyed the lives of our people.* Passive: *Our repeated Petitions have been answered only by repeated injury.*

Is it possible to edit too deeply?

Yes, and if you do, you'll know it in three ways. First, you'll get questions from the reader because you've left out something essential.

A great plan, but it fails to mention when we start, or who's involved...

Second, you will find that your investment in time is greater than the benefit in brevity. If you spend 30 minutes to shorten a two-paragraph message, it's probably not a good investment of time. Remember that we work mostly in an 8-1/2 by 11 space.

Third, your over-edited writing will simply sound odd—too telegraphic and offensive to the mind's ear. Sometimes those little connectors we're removing serve to lubricate the language and should be left alone.

More Tips

Avoid vague modifiers.

Very, quite and *slightly* tend to disarm an otherwise strong message.

Slightly behind schedule is better as *a day and a half late*.

Very upset probably means *angry* or *furious*.

Some painted surfaces are not quite up to standard takes on clearer meaning as *three out of five are scratched*.

You might not be understood with *Substantial additions will have to be made in order to meet our needs*, so you change it to *We'll require forty percent more parts*.

Watch the roundabouts.

In their attempts to appear erudite, some executives imitate what they see as British reserve by selecting roundabout constructions.

This situation is not unlike one we've had in the past...

I wouldn't disagree with the view that...
I wouldn't be doing my job if I didn't say... and so forth.

These can be particularly troublesome when translated into other languages. Watch out if your writing is going to someone whose first language is other than English.

Focus on the reader.

Don't focus on the writer; point out the benefits the reader will realize from your product or project.

Most readers care little about:

> *we have done this for you...*
> *overcame these obstacles...*
> *achievements despite reverses...*
> *snatching victory ...*

But, a reader should want to know:

> *you will be seeing results from...*
> *this will improve your...*
> *this can help you save as much as...*
> and *your customers soon will see...*

The "struggling upward" stuff about how you've knocked yourself out for the reader wears very thin, very fast.

Are we humble?

Be careful of questionable humility. The obsequious tone of *respectfully submitted* and similar constructions introduces characteristics in you, the chief executive, that others would rather not see. What's more, Americans' habit of ever-so-profusely thanking customers for doing business with us makes our *thank you very much* a low-value currency. (Perhaps you've noticed that the words are the same for the purchase of a pack of gum or a luxury sedan).

It's better to compliment the customer on his or her judgment and taste than to offer idle thanks. *Our engineers agree that you're going to look back on this as a wise choice.*

Write positively.

Oh, how hard we try to drive away customers!

The sale will end promptly at midnight on Friday, when prices will be raised. Why not: *You can take advantage of these great savings all the way up to midnight on Friday!*

Or, why is it written as *You didn't give me enough information in your letter, so I don't know if I can help you...* instead of *Please let me have a little more information, so I can help you better.*

And whoever wrote *Do not jam the lid shut with a lot of force, or you might break off the little safety clips* probably should have added, *you jerk!*

A proper translation might be, *Please close the lid carefully to protect the safety clips.*

Trapping the reader into a short list of unacceptable choices can make blood boil, too, as in:

You have just two choices: either use the product the way it is, or return it for credit against your next purchase.

To this, the reader probably adds a third option having to do with putting that product in your ear. Better choices: *Let me suggest a couple of options...* or, *There are several ways I can help you.*

The message: Before you lick the stamp or start the speech, re-read your material to see if it's a properly positive message you are sending.

What language is this?

Some executives feel the need to insert foreign words into their writings—*elan* instead of *dash,* for example, or *kaizen* instead of *continuous improvement.* Although this may be an attempt to inform the reader that one has been to school or traveled abroad, it's fraught with dangers. I have numerous scars attesting to my wrongheaded attempts to communicate in Japanese. Usually, these are caused by my being unaware of second and third meanings of common Japanese words.

The word *kami,* for example, can refer to paper, to hair or to a divinity—offering ample opportunities to foul up or to give offense.

English is a marvelously broad and deep language, with many more words in active use than, say, French or German. It offers countless opportunities to convey many levels of meaning. So, you needn't insert foreign words into your writing.

My suggestion: use foreign words <u>only</u> if:

a. you cannot find a way to say it in English;
b. you are absolutely certain you will be understood; and
c. you are as good at that language as the reader.

Use short sentences, short words.

Another way to show that you've been to school is the use of polysyllabic words, perhaps on the theory that the longer one's words, the greater one's education. That's nonsense, of course. Ordinary words carry all the meaning that's required, and in fact the shortest—those from the Anglo-Saxon side of our vocabulary—are among the most forceful.

Think about the proverbs we learned as children, all presented memorably in words of one syllable:

> *Where there's a will, there's a way.*
> *A stitch in time saves nine.*
> *Spare the rod and spoil the child.*
> *A bird in the hand is worth two in the bush.*

Word From the Top
The Chief Executive's Guide to Business Communication

Winston Churchill, a gifted writer and orator, chose one-syllable words to explain the plan for dealing with his nation's enemies: *I will say: it is to wage war by sea, land, and air, with all our might and with all the strength that God can give us.*

And John Kennedy used but a single two-syllable word in one of his most famous deliveries: *Ask not what your country can do for you; ask what you can do for your country.*

Most short words seem fresh, neat, crisp and clear. And most of them can say what you mean with much more ease and grace than large words. Great men have told of wars and toil, fears and death, of their loves lost and their lives spent in pain. They told it all and caught our ears with a nest of small words that would fit in your hand. Those good words come from a time when work was hard and life was coarse and plain—a time when all who had a need to speak were more wise with words, and so used only a few. These were so brief, they came and went in the blink of an eye.

Say and write what you mean with the old, quick words that the folks spoke at home. Write to a friend. Tell of the good times, fun times, of your work, your hopes, your joys, your aims, your dreams. Say how it feels to be in love, how to pity, how to feel sad. Write not with your hand, but with your heart. Put these good, small words to use each day at home, at play or on the job. They want to shine in use, not turn dull and dark with age.

The preceding two paragraphs, had you not noticed, are written in one-syllable words.

Don't bother reaching for language; the best of it is well within your grasp.

The Outline

An outline can take much of the struggle out of business writing. That said, the kind of outline makes a big difference.

The kind Sister Mary showed us when we were in grade school made a lot of sense as outlines, but they're difficult to convert into text. This we've found to be true all the way through our educational experience as we swung from term paper to term paper, all based on the Roman numeraled outlines: *I, A, 1, a*, and so forth.

This system's failing is that it's linear—like trying to find something on a videotape that has to be played end to end. It demands you remember that to put an "A" on the outline you must first know that there will be a "B."

Idea clusters

A better system is what I call "idea clusters," which is more like finding files on a computer's hard drive. This is akin to what others call "mind mapping." Simply throw ideas at the paper by writing key subjects as they occur to you, in no order at all, perhaps putting them into balloons.

Then list subsidiary topics under these and indicate where borrowed material may be inserted from other media: You indicate *Insert A* under

Distribution, for example, or *Copy from news release* under *Facilities*. All that's left is to number the headings and start to write.

You'll wonder why you haven't been outlining this way all along.

In drafting your letter for the annual report, for example, your main topics might be *Results, Labor relations, Capitalization, Management changes, New facilities, Cost controls, Acquisition initiatives, Economic environment, Markets, Environmental affairs* and *Product development*. Adding a few bullets under each and then putting them in order by numbering major items takes only a moment.

How to organize it

But <u>which</u> order? That depends on the message. The old, reliable way is the one journalists use—from most to least important. This makes the work easy to edit; chop material beginning at the bottom and you may lose some detail, but not the main point.

Or, thesis style: State your case and provide backup for it. *We must buy or build a plant in the Southeast.* Then, deal with the market, shipping costs, labor costs, plant capacity and the rest.

You might organize your work chronologically. This can be useful if you're reporting on a chain of events or a succession of stops on a trip.

Some written work is organized according to a "logic flow." It's the "if-then" way.

If we enlarge the Dallas facility, we'll ease the overload in Cleveland and that, in turn, will make space available in Detroit.

Perhaps the most useful is the form of organization based on an acronym—AIDA. Attention, Interest, Desire, Action. It's particularly useful in messages to persuade, as in selling or advertising.

Use some device to create <u>attention</u>: *Hey, your car's on fire!*

Then, build <u>interest</u> by describing features: *We have four ways to put out that annoying fire in your car. We have a garden hose; an asbestos blanket; a bucket of sand; and a fire extinguisher.*

Next, build <u>desire</u> by presenting benefits: *Our asbestos blanket is the least costly, but also the least effective. The bucket of sand works better, and costs slightly more, but it leaves a horrid mess in your car. The garden hose is faster, but it, too, leaves your upholstery soggy. Your best choice could be our fire extinguisher; its higher cost is more than offset by its speed, and it leaves no residue.*

Finally, move the reader to <u>action</u>: *This new fire extinguisher will have that fire out in minutes, and the manufacturer is offering big rebates for this month only.*

Your message might be organized this way:

We're spending tens of thousands needlessly on this equipment each year. Any of the three leasing programs available could save us a lot—A, B or C. A is easiest to administer...B requires less up-front. I recommend C, which involves the lowest cost and the most convenience. If we act before the end of this month, we can save...

If you pay attention to television commercials and full-page newspaper ads, you'll see this style at work almost every day.

When to Write

A noted horticulturist was asked about the right time to prune a certain species of tree. He said, "I'd prune it when the saw is sharp," suggesting that the season doesn't make a difference.

The corollary in writing is, *write when you have the information*, and not a moment later. Information stored in our brains is notoriously perishable, so it's important to get something on paper right away. If you're at the wheel of your car, dictate it into a machine or note it in the margin of your newspaper. Almost any method of saving this moment's idea will be helpful later on.

What time of day? I suggest early morning. Even if you're not a morning person, you'll be physically refreshed then, and you won't be the product of a whole day's emotional ups and downs. If during the day you have to discharge a long-time employee, face bad news from your financial people, receive a summons, or have some other negative experience, you'll be in no shape to create any messages at four o'clock. Wait 'till tomorrow.

It's important to know your mood, too. If you have unpleasant duties ahead, or if there's something under your skin, it's best to wait until that's cleared before you write.

A word about booze. It might feel good to slither into a big chair in your living room with a pen in one hand and a bourbon in the other, ready to face the annual message to shareholders. But be careful. That stuff may make you feel more creative, but it's not as good as it will make you believe. Be sure to read that report again first thing in the morning, before you hand it off.

Find a Reviewer

Because you run the place, it may be hard to find someone who won't flatter your socks off about what a great writer you are. But it's important to try. I suggest tapping people at several levels in the company, so you're not hearing the same song from everyone.

You might be surprised, for example, to get the perspective of a receptionist or a field salesperson, or a supervisor on the factory floor.

At least one company apparently didn't do enough of this. A worker who read the annual report in the bindery lunchroom pointed out that it wasn't really the company's 50th anniversary after all—it was the 49th.

How to Stay Fresh

We're mimics, most of us, and we try to imitate the best writers. This being true, we should go where the best writers are and read what they write.

If you have time to read only one periodical, make it *The Wall Street Journal*. This remarkable paper represents the nation's best business journalism, written and edited under severe deadline pressure. What the *Journal* does best is what all business writers need to learn better: how to define and describe.

Go to an article on a subject you know nothing about, and in the second or third paragraph you're likely to find a very tightly written, highly polished description.

One *Wall Street Journal* writer described *short sales* this way:

"Short-sellers borrow shares, usually from brokerage houses or institutions, and immediately sell them. They eventually have to purchase the stock to return to the lender, and they profit if the stock price has fallen in the meantime."

Another did it like this:

"A short sale is a bet that a stock will decline. Short sellers borrow shares and immediately sell them. Eventually, they must buy shares to replace the borrowed ones, but if the stock drops in the meantime, they profit."

And a third said:

> "Short-selling is the sale of borrowed stock in hopes of a price decline; the idea is to return cheaper shares to the lender."

If you want one-stop shopping for a business writing and editing model, *The Wall Street Journal* is the place to go.

About E-Mail

Executives have told me that the quality of writing is pretty good in the letters, plans, memos and reports their people write. But most agree that the quality of e-mail communications is lousy.

I'm amused to hear people say, "I don't write much any more; I use e-mail."

It does seem that we turn off the rules when we communicate electronically. That's too bad, because this wonderful medium gives us the chance to move huge amounts of information very quickly and to get almost instantaneous response from the reader.

The principal failing appears to be a lack of editing. Writers seem emboldened to write long, rambling streams of words and then hurriedly hit the "Send" button.

What's required are reminders that the only thing different about e-mail is that it's fast, and that e-mail messages should be edited as carefully as those delivered on paper.

Here's a suggestion: Remind all employees that high writing standards should be maintained when using e-mail *because electronic communications are company property, available for review by anyone, including the chief executive.*

This will improve the quality of e-mail messages. As a corollary benefit, you'll see a huge drop in the volume of personal messages and non-business website hits.

The Annual Report

For some reason, corporate executives and more than a few writers make a much bigger deal of writing the annual report than this project requires. We know we have to produce it, we know what the facts are, we know how we feel about the future. So, let's get on with it.

I can't think of a situation that would require more than a two-page chief executive's letter in the annual report. I note, however, that in many letters the first three paragraphs are taken up by a repetition of the tabular material in the financial highlights. Page fright, I suppose.

Put the numbers in front of you and crack into the job by telling the shareholder (Remember, we'll picture just one, right?) what happened last year, and why the numbers look like that. Then explain the changes you've made, make a word picture of the company's general situation and financial condition, detail any important appointments or other news of the year, and end up with something about your markets and outlook.

What happened, why, what you did about it, how the company looks at year's end, and what you see ahead. Simple, really.

Common Mistakes

Chief executives' messages in annual reports fall into a kind of rhythm, suggesting that everyone who writes one is reading everyone else's. Readers can be put off by habits that are repeated from one company's annual report to another.

Assuming continuity of readership.

As we said in last year's annual report...

(I didn't read it)

As stated in the company's standards of business conduct...

(I haven't seen it)

As we have said for the past three years...

(Sorry, I just heard about the company)

As expected, earnings were affected by...

(Really? I guess I missed the forecast).

It's best to assume the reader is new. Tell the whole story without referring to documents that the reader may not have at hand.

The feature edition.

Telling the whole story every year means you'll inform every reader every time. If the report features, say, international operations (Photo caption: Board members view Eiffel Tower), you'll be drawing attention to one side of the business and creating a picture that doesn't fully reflect the company. This kind of report, too, assumes the readers know the company well enough to look forward to this year's feature. In fact, given everything else that's going on in the market, we're lucky to get them to pick the report up and look at it.

Inconsistent or confusing nomenclature.

The Ball Bearing Division, The Consumer Division, The Fuszard Division and *The California Group* refer to a product, a market, a family name and a place. Confusing? Yes, and it's easy to fix. You needn't change the nomenclature of the organization—just communicate the company's operations consistently by market, by product, by trade name or by geography. And not all at once.

Hanging a dead man.

Mentioning all the sins of our corporate forebears gets very old, very fast. Repeated references to the mess our management team inherited from the previous one, instead of explanations of how we're fixing it, may suggest we don't know how.

At some point, present management has to be accountable. That's us, Boss.

What, blame me?

Many CEO letters place blame squarely in one direction: away from management.

Forces beyond our control... unscrupulous competitors... government interference... unseasonable weather... intransigent union... cheap imports... disgruntled former employees... and so on.

Yes, stuff happens, but at some point, present management must accept responsibility. The best-regarded managements are those that step up and say, *We misread the economic signals...*or, *In making our plans we simply didn't consider...*

Readers are amazingly forgiving of honest mistakes, provided they're acknowledged with honest answers.

Your naughty company.

Ever read a stack of annual reports from one company and find that its ownership seems to change depending on its results?

In good times:*We made good progress last year...* or, *Our company achieved excellent results...*

But in adversity: *Your company failed to realize its promise...* or, *Your company's results last year were unacceptable.*

Funny—the company that was *ours* became *yours* when things went to hell.

My mom loves me.

Some writers turn to the "golly-gosh" syndrome to paint the chief executive as so warm and wonderful, nobody could criticize his or her performance.

Grace, a grandmother who's been with us for more than thirty years...

- or -

Ernie, our irrepressible maintenance man...

It doesn't work if the performance is missing. And it makes analysts retch.

Wow, are we green!

Recycling all our office papers...

- or -

Aluminum-can collection points in every cafeteria...

Excuse me, but everybody is doing this, and it's our job. And if we take credit for recycling corrugated paperboard when everybody else in our industry is using returnable containers, we'll look like fools. So be absolutely sure the company has a good and complete record on environmental matters, or don't make the claim.

And be sure you understand the technology involved before you beat that drum too hard.

Too hip.

If you read only corporate annual reports, you'll speak an unusual language. They've become catch-basins for euphemisms, techno-babble and hot-stuff bizspeak. Remember *paradigm shifts* from a few years ago? By the time most readers figured out what that meant, it wasn't used any more.

And just as the "hot stuff" changes from year to year, so do the euphemisms. *Layoff* is nixed in favor of *redeployment, rightsizing, production adjustment* and dozens of other choices. Perhaps we've learned all this from government, where *revenue enhancement* has come to replace *tax increase.*

Ordinary language works, and ordinary people understand it.

The bottom line.

Shareholders, analysts, bankers and the others who read annual reports are pretty smart. They'll forgive almost anything except lying and outright theft. Write to them in adult language, acknowledging mistakes and taking full credit for the good work you've done. Address them as you would your next-door neighbors and you'll hit it about right. They just might *be* your next-door neighbors.

Managing Writers

You are lucky if you have someone on staff to help you with writing, and luckier still if that person gives you straight talk about the company's messages. If that writer is too deferential to your rank, you won't get honest answers. If he or she is capable of telling you that something you've written is a load of crap (in gentler language, one hopes), you have a genuine asset.

Getting the best from the people who write for you requires a little handling. Here are some ideas:

What you reward is what you get

If you reward poor writing by allowing it to continue, it will continue. The people who work for you are smart, but if they think you want bushels of words and lots of embroidery on your writing, that's what you'll get. Just tell them what you want. Once should do it.

Of course, rewarding the good writing will earn more of that for you, too.

Set some standards

Try these:

> *I want to keep all our communications to one page if possible.*
>
> *- and -*
>
> *Don't put unnecessary detail into your written work; if I need more, I'll ask for it.*
>
> *- and -*
>
> *Show me your outlines early; I'll give you my input right away.*

Issue clear, complete instructions

Your people are good, but they aren't mindreaders.

He says a few words about it and then walks away.

- or -

I could have done this in one paragraph or in three pages; the safe way was three pages, and he hit the roof.

The relationship with your writer has to be two-way, so take a moment and explain what you want. They can't do it right without you.

Set a good example

Does this mean the chief executive has to be the best writer in the place? No, it almost never happens that way. Set an example by <u>caring</u> about the kind of written work that's produced.

I've heard employees say, *My boss can't even read, let alone write. You can put any piece of junk in front of him and he'll sign it.*

If the boss doesn't care, why should they?

Do some editing

If you take just a few moments to change some things that have been written for you, the writer will learn very quickly what you want. Odds are, you'll never have to make that kind of correction again. And if you have an extra moment, explain <u>why</u>.

The least-productive thing you can do with a draft is indicate *Don't like this...* or *Not your best effort...* or *Is this the best we can do?* They tell the writer nothing except that you're dissatisfied.

Make some changes and hand it back.

Don't nitpick

Nothing is more disheartening to a writer.

> *I don't spend much time on it any more, since I know he'll just tear it apart and do his own thing anyway.*
>
> - or -
>
> *He's putting things into the third draft that he took out of the first one.*

Is that upsetting to the writer? Yes, it might make him want to choke the life out of you. When you're tempted to change something, ask yourself, *Do the changes I'm suggesting make this product better, or just different?*

Expect and accept an assertive attitude

Your writers should be speaking up with comments such as, *Sorry, but I can't perform with the information I have here; please tell me more.*

They should question you until they understand fully.

###

Thomas E. Fuszard

The Spoken Word

Introduction

I like to begin my presentation-skills coaching by quizzing the participants about their feelings on public speaking. I ask, "How many of you love to speak in public, and do it as often as you can?" One hand might go up, more often none, from a typical group of a dozen.

Then I ask, "How many would rather do almost anything else?" This gets most of the hands in the air.

Finally I ask, "How many would rather *die*?" Most hands, again.

In fact, public speaking ranks much higher than death on surveys of Americans' worst fears. It usually finishes first.

When I ask senior executives if they're nervous about public speaking, they generally say, "Well, you know, I've done quite a lot of this," which leaves my question largely unanswered.

For the moment, let's agree that all of us are at least a little apprehensive about our speaking assignments. Maybe I can help with an idea, suggestion, reminder—something that will help you be more effective, more forceful and more comfortable.

Thomas E. Fuszard

Three Types of Presentations

American businesspeople make vocal presentations mainly in three formats: formal speeches; small-group presentations; and one-on-one conversations, usually to sell a product or service.

Arranging these in order of difficulty for the speaker, the one-on-one pitch to make a sale or arrange a deal is at the top. Yes, you're talking to just one person, but you have that person's undivided attention and cannot escape his or her eyes. What's more, you probably have a lot riding on this presentation, and you're unlikely to get another shot at this prospect on this subject. So, the cost of failure is high. That means the stress level is high.

Next down the scale of difficulty is the small-group presentation. This is the meeting, often impromptu, at which you're talking to three or five or ten people for three or five or ten minutes. You may have had little or no warning, as when you return from vacation a day early and someone, suddenly finding you available, asks you to speak to a group of new hires or to some people just completing a training program.

You have ten minutes to prepare and ten minutes to be wonderful.

Easiest of all is the formal speech, although many executives think I have my arrangement backwards. The speech invariably gives you time to prepare, and you generally have people to help. Somebody may draft your remarks, someone else edits it, others review it and put it into final form. But even if you must do it all yourself, you'll have plenty of time to review it and rehearse it, perhaps in front of others or in front of a television camera.

By the time you stand up to deliver a speech, you should be so thoroughly prepared you could do it in your sleep. That's why I call this the easiest format of all. It's an 80/20 thing: the speech is 80 percent preparation, 20 percent speaker's presence; a small-group presentation is 20 percent preparation and 80 percent *you*.

Stage Fright

Know these feelings? Dry mouth, sweaty palms, shallow breathing, sinking stomach, tightness in the throat, panic attack…

Most of us hate to hear an instructor or coach tell us this fear is natural and useful, and that it spurs us on to greater achievement. We think, *that might work for you, pal, but I'm in trouble here.* In fact, a little apprehension does tend to sharpen our focus, making us more attentive and intense. It's the fight-or-flight impulse that helped our ancestors overcome danger, or flee from it, so they could continue the bloodline.

Think about why we're afraid:

I probably will be embarrassed.
They won't like what I'm wearing.
I might look silly or sound stupid.
Somebody will know this stuff better than I do.
Everybody is looking at me.

Those are lousy reasons to be afraid. The only good reason to be afraid is that <u>they won't get your message</u>—that your presentation will be a flop because you've not prepared, and you will waste everyone's time.

When we stand before an audience, we think we know what they're thinking:

> *This guy is a jerk.*
> *He seems nervous and tense.*
> *He's a really poor presenter.*
> *I feel embarrassed for him.*

Want to know what they're actually thinking? It's probably something more like:

> *I forgot to buy a gift for my mother.*
> *I don't know what to do about all my bills.*
> *Think I'll ask the boss for more money.*
> *I wonder who won the football pool.*
> *I feel awful; I wonder if that shrimp I ate was okay.*

The bottom line is that most people in most audiences probably don't care about what you have to say. You have to make them care. So, don't worry about being afraid; worry about not getting your message across. That's a proper reason to crank up your anxiety level.

Dealing With Stage Fright

Remember that you are the expert.

You are here either because you are the person steering this ship or because someone figured you are the one person on staff who knows the most about this issue or situation. It will ease your anxiety a lot to bear in mind that you have the facts—more of them than anyone else. If you're there because you are the chief executive, people will expect a lot of you…but they'll accept a lot, too. They don't want you to fail.

Remember that they need to hear what you have to say.

Not only are you the expert, but you have a message that's useful if not essential to the audience. What you tell them will help them perform better, make more money, be successful…

Remember that your nervousness doesn't show.

The audience can't see that your mouth is dry, or that your palms are sweaty. They can't see the sinking feeling in your midsection. They will observe your nervousness only if:

a. you grip the edge of the lectern so hard your knuckles turn white;

b. you allow your limbs to stiffen so your movements become robotic and mechanical; or

c. you point to a screen or, worse, to a transparency on a projector with a pointer, which magnifies the trembling of your hand. (Suggestions: press the pointer against the screen or transparency so it doesn't shake, or point with your finger. If you must use a pointer, try holding it in your left hand if you're right-handed; many people find that for some reason they tremble much less this way.)

Preview the audience.

Literally, that is. If you get the chance between the presentations that precede yours, go to the front of the meeting room and take a look at the audience from there. If you've been a part of the audience for a while, and then rise to speak to them, that friendly bunch you've been looking at from the back or side can seem menacing when you face them.

My long-time friend, a well-known graphic designer, was at a convention where the association chairman asked him to stop by the ballroom to say a few words to some of the members later that afternoon. He showed up and chatted with a dozen or so members at a bar that was set up in one end of the room. Then, the chairman asked him to address the group. My friend turned and saw that while he had been talking, several hundred people had gathered to hear him speak. He said his stomach sank into his lizard boots, and it took several minutes to compose himself before he could put sensible sentences together. That agony could have been avoided had he paid attention to the group assembling in the hall.

Greeting audience members as they arrive is a great way to relieve your anxieties.

Stand up.

If possible, get on your feet and move into position so that when you're introduced, you will be able to take a couple of steps and begin to speak. If you rise to speak from a sitting position, the adrenaline rush may make you feel light-headed or woozy. Get up as early as you can and get your body jangled into a posture that's ready for delivery.

Grab something tangible.

Handling something while you begin to speak—a sample product, a scale model, a book, a pen, a pointer—can help defuse tension. But be careful to handle the object for a short time and then put it down or pass it around. Don't stand there fiddling with it; that drives the audience nuts.

Rehearse or die.

If you have so much confidence that you feel you never have to rehearse a speech or presentation, you're one in a million. And if you are certain that the disk drive in your head will never go blank in mid-presentation, you are dead wrong. I've never met an executive who didn't have at least one horror story about losing his or her place in a speech, or simply going blank. All the best speakers rehearse again and again.

The way to do it is to do it.

Books, training classes, coaching and rehearsals can be very helpful. But the only way to get better at this stuff is to put it to work in front of a live audience. Get yourself in front of groups as often as you can. The practice will keep you fresh. It's a skill that needs to be polished.

Remember that it only lasts two minutes.

Any physical manifestations of nervousness disappear like magic about two minutes into your presentation. I've seen it innumerable times in training classes: a speaker's arm and leg joints are locked, creating mechanical, robot-like movements; then, right at the two-minute mark, the joints are unlocked and gestures become fluid and natural.

Many of the best speakers seem to sense this. They do something to burn that two-minute nervousness fuse. Think about trade-association convention keynoters, for example, and how many of them begin: *As we start, I'd like to take a minute to recognize one of your members who's a long-time friend and rival. Bill Smith and I have been competitors for more than twenty years, and I've always admired him for his fairness and honest dealings. He's a tough competitor who doesn't give me an inch, but Bill always maintains the highest standards of professional practice. Your association is lucky to have him as a member.*

What the speaker has done is ingratiate himself with the audience by fondly acknowledging one of their members. He's made himself appear sensitive and human. But most important, he's burned off a couple of minutes' worth of nervousness. Now, he's ready to begin.

Watch any President of the United States as he prepares to deliver the State of the Union address. He's introduced from the rear of the chamber and moves forward, shaking hands. He ascends the podium and shakes hands with the Speaker of the House and the Vice President. But does he begin to speak immediately? No. He chats briefly with these two as though he'd not seen them for some time. Then, the President turns to address the Congress.

Is this just a habit or custom, or a deliberate effort to burn off two minutes of nervousness? I don't know, but it seems to work.

Moving Your Message

Studies indicate that audiences retain much less of what we tell them than we would like—perhaps half of a luncheon presentation by dinnertime and only a tiny fraction of it by the end of the week. Knowing that information stored in the audience brain mass is notoriously perishable, you have three possibilities as you attack this information leakage:

1. get them to remember *more* of what you say;
2. get them to remember what you say *longer*; and,
3. get them to remember *what you want them to remember*.

We know the audience won't remember all of what we say, or for long. The best we can do is to get them to remember a few key points. This we do by building some peaks or spikes into the content—something memorable, along the lines of television sound bites.

Getting Ready

Thomas E. Fuszard

A few moments' thought about the presentation you're preparing can be immensely helpful in organizing your ideas. I recommend a kind of step-by-step procedure in which you ask yourself a number of questions.

The Mission

Who are you trying to reach, and what do you want them to do? Just as in writing, it's important to put aside all the extraneous stuff, such as how long the message should be.

I'm asked to speak to a group of our principal suppliers, leading off a conference on product quality. What I want them to do is carry away the message that we will do whatever is necessary to help them meet our standards for incoming parts and materials. I want them to spread that message throughout engineering, design, sales—every part of their companies, so everybody will be on the same page when it comes to quality. We're raising the bar and we want them all to make it.

The Assignment

Who asked you to make the presentation? Why should it be you? Is it because of your rank, or because of your experience with this situation, problem, product or operation? Why now?

The answers should help you fit into the role of speaker, enabling you to visualize the situation and helping you to feel comfortable with it.

The Audience

Who are they, by profession or role? What is their relationship to you or your organization? What do they know about the subject? How important is it to them? Why do they *need* to know about it?

It's a big help, finding out who they are and what's on their minds. Oddly, however, many speakers accept engagements without asking much about the audience. Perhaps this is why so many messages miss the mark as speakers talk over the heads of listeners, or sound like teachers in front of a first-grade class.

It costs nothing to ask. Just call them up.

I'm delighted to be asked to speak to your group. Please take a minute and let me know what you think is on their minds...any hot current issues...concerns you've heard expressed...

The Messages

A picture will begin to form in your mind. You'll begin to sort ideas into two or three messages you will want to pass on. That's usually as many as you can expect the audience to keep in mind.

As you think about each message, you might also begin thinking about the best way to illustrate or explain each one, if that's a possibility given the proposed setting.

An interesting new product? I'll distribute samples. A safety issue? I could use that three-minute video showing the testing process. Environmental problems? Perhaps the slides showing improvements in the recovery and reclamation process.

You're well on your way.

The Expectation

Deciding on a reasonable expectation from your presentation is an important part of this quick little planning process. It's important because it can help gear your presentation to a logical, likely outcome that will not disappoint you.

Talking to a group that includes some of your biggest customers, for example, would it be reasonable to expect them to rush forward when you finish, clamoring for the chance to order your product? Of course not. If you have anything like that in mind, you will see your presentation as a failure. But if you can get some of them nodding and elbowing each other, and if the discussion later indicates that they're impressed and excited, your presentation worked. And you are a winner.

Following your presentation to a supplier group, would it be reasonable to expect an immediate, 20 percent improvement in the quality of purchased parts? No. But if you expect the audience to react favorably to your message, and later hear them say they'll be forming teams with your people on quality assurance, you've won.

The point is to aim high, but only high enough so you can reasonably expect to succeed in moving your message. Set the expectation too high and you'll set yourself up for failure.

Staying in Control

Here are some thoughts about improving your presentation skills—ways to help you look and sound prepared, professional and confident.

Be prepared.

This is simple stuff, but be sure you've thought about notes or a script, materials you may be needing, audio/visual aids, and all the other homework that's required. Give yourself time to relax and refresh yourself before your presentation.

Do some *visualization* of the event that's ahead, picturing in your mind's eye how you will be introduced, how you'll behave in front of the audience, how you will win them over, how you'll handle questions, how you will finish strongly.

It's positive imaging; if you're a golfer or world-class athlete, this process should be nothing new to you.

Give them a reason to care.

Remember radio station WII-FM: What's In It For Me. Tell your audience why you're talking to them. How you're going to help them make a profit, avoid a loss, be spared embarrassment...

Don't be afraid to tell the audience why it's important—how it relates to the future of the company, the department, the project, the individual's career.

Explain why they're being told this *now*. Perhaps some information is needed urgently to stop losses, correct a problem, prepare for an event.

Most people aren't prepared to give a damn about what you have to say. You may have to tell them why they should care.

Set the schedule.

A sure-fire way to get and keep the audience's attention is to tell them how long they will be sitting there. Think about it: as we enter most meeting rooms, aren't we a little apprehensive about how long the meeting will last? We look around to see who else is there; we check the materials being handed out; we count slides in a projector.

Sometimes an audience begins muttering after ten minutes or so:

He's on slide two, and there are fifty slides; we're gonna be here all day.

- or -

He's only passed out two of those big folders, and there are eight more to go. I think we're stuck.

Don't make the audience wonder. Try something like this:

I need no more than twelve minutes to explain this program.

- or -

We will be here no later than nine-thirty.

- or -

In the next 20 minutes, I will show you how to save...

This relieves the concern that the meeting will consume huge amounts of time. It also shows that you're organized. You'll probably see people looking at their watches to note the time, just to see if you can make it under the limit you've imposed on yourself.

One other thing: it can help to un-round the time. Telling an audience that they will be engaged for a half hour can mean to some of them that it's okay to turn off their brains for a while. But telling them that your message needs 27 minutes is like issuing a challenge. You'll be listened to, and of course everyone will check you on the time.

At least that means you have them engaged.

Surprise them with your brevity.

Picture a speaker who talks to your group forcefully and a bit rapidly, then finishes early and sits down. If you're like most people, you see someone like that as well organized, well informed and probably quite bright.

Trouble is, there are too few like that in the American business community. We might be good presenters, but few of us know when to shut up and sit down.

If you have 15 minutes on the meeting agenda, use 10. Force yourself to compress that presentation, removing all the trash—just as you will be doing with your written work. And if that works well in writing, it works even better with speech.

Can you remember whose keynote speech preceded Lincoln's 267-word Gettysburg Address? Neither can anyone else—not what was said or who said it. For the record, it was Edward Everett (professor, congressman, senator, governor, cabinet member, ambassador, vice-presidential candidate, Harvard president), who was said to be a superb orator. He talked for two hours; Lincoln did his in three or four minutes.

Organize for power

You're trying to be remembered, so put your material into a form that helps the audience's recall. One way is to use the forceful AIDA format mentioned in the section on writing skills. It works beautifully in vocal presentations.

Attention: *At the present rate, our European operations will be out of cash in less than six months.*

Interest: *We can consolidate operations into three centers... discontinue our activities in Italy...and replace costly local designs with U.S.-engineered products.*

Desire: *Here's how each of these changes will benefit operations...*

Action: *We can save the ship. But we need to start today, right now.*

Don't share your outline

Telling your audience why they are there, and what you plan to discuss, is enough. There is no need to share your outline. If you do, the rapid readers will skim ahead and tune you out. Others will groan when you spend a long time on the first item or two, figuring they'll be trapped there for hours.

The same is true of any printed material you plan to distribute. Do that when you've finished talking. If it is essential that the audience follow along with some printed piece, put it on the screen in slide, slick or PowerPoint form so *you* can stay in control of the pacing. And keep it quick, please.

Start strong

Memorizing your first three or four lines is a proven device for limiting stage fright and helping you to sound organized and confident. By itself, that will get your audience's attention.

A strong statement: *Half the customers we sold last year will never do business with us again.*

A question: *Have you ever wondered how many of our new customers will stay with us?*

A statistic: *One-third of all Americans—a total of some 90 million people—believe that...*

A quotation: *The founder of our parent company used to say...*

An anecdote: *Three cave dwellers had a problem like ours back in 1500 B.C. One of them said to the others, ...*

By the way, if you've memorized those first three or four lines, be sure to carry them on a card or pad just in case you go blank as you rise to speak.

Keep it light

Humor can help humanize the speaker and establish a bond with the audience. It also loosens you up, especially if you draw a laugh early in your remarks. If after a couple of minutes someone says to his neighbor, "I think this guy is gonna be okay," you're ahead of the game.

So, humor works better with the spoken word than in business writing, but all the cautions are the same: nothing racial, religious, ethnic, political, sexist, sexual…

Stay with self-effacing humor. Aim those barbs your own way and you'll be fine.

Here's another caution: Watch out for the "big-bang" jokes. They're those long stories that usually begin, *There were these three guys. One of them was a…*

It's tough to win with these. For one thing, you probably borrowed the story, so you're not as familiar with it as if you'd written one yourself. So, your delivery may be shaky. Worse, you might drop the punch line too early, or deliver it poorly at the end. That will have people in the audience turning to one another, asking, "What did he say?"

That's a rotten way to start.

Enumerate.

Here's another method that works even better in vocal presentations than on paper. Early in your remarks, you can alert the audience to your little litany of problems, opportunities, places, things.

I have four simple suggestions to make you a better presenter.

> - or -
>
> *By following three rules, we can maintain this pace.*
>
> - or -
>
> *Five competitors dominate this business, and all five are in trouble.*

You should hear the ball-point pens click when you say this. Then, you'll have the audience's attention until you finish the list. It's simple and it works.

Make statements in question form.

Vary your vocal presentations so your audience hears an occasional question from you, not simply a long list of declarative sentences.

> *Did you ever ask yourself if there's another way to fix the XYZ?*
>
> - or -
>
> *Why do you suppose management arranged it that way?*
>
> - or -
>
> *Haven't we all wished we could change it somehow?*

These rhetorical questions change the tone of your presentation and gently challenge your listeners to think, or at least to remain alert.

Solicit a response.

Even better is the question that calls for a response.

Thomas E. Fuszard

How many of you watched that TV documentary last night?

- or -

Does anyone have an opinion about how this works?

- or -

Have any of you had experience with equipment like this?

Almost any question you ask an audience will stir attention and keep the focus on your presentation. Any question, that is, except "Anybody have a question?" That's weak, and no one wants to speak up for fear of delaying the presentation and detaining the group.

Say it and write it.

In your informal presentations, you can improve the memorability of what you say by writing it as you say it. The audience will be drawn to your writing, and will acquire what you say both visually and aurally. A multi-media presentation, if you wish.

Get <u>them</u> to write it.

Most presenters are so polite, they cannot bring themselves to ask an audience to take note of something. Too bad; it's a great way to help people remember. Now they're seeing it, hearing it and writing it. Your chances of being remembered, at least for the items they've written down, are pretty good.

If you remember nothing else from today, please make a note of this.

- or -

Please write this down, and look at it again in a week.

- or -

I'd love to have you write these three brief reminders.

Say it with pictures.

Adding any kind of picture to your presentation will improve understanding and memorability—a slide, a slick, a graph, a photograph, perhaps a map. And although it seems odd, a crude picture that you draw on a flip chart or an overhead transparency will have greater memorability than a carefully done mechanical drawing that you put on the screen.

Next time you see a streetcorner caricature artist at work, watch the crowd around him. You'll see every eye glued to the work as his hand moves. The same is true in your meeting room. Make the sketch in front of the audience and it's likely to be remembered.

Move!

Get away from the lectern when you can, and move about from time to time. This varies the scene for the eyes of the audience, making it a little easier to keep their attention. It changes the angle of the sound of your voice, too, and that serves to keep attention.

Best of all, a little motion will help you relax. Walk slowly across the front of the room, talking as you move; stop for a while, then move again. It's a marvelous way to relieve stage fright, especially early in your presentation.

Jog distracted listeners

Audience members who are nodding off, or those who whisper incessantly to their neighbors, are very distracting for others in the group. So, you needn't worry about being impolite when you jog them back into your presentation. Just mentioning their names is usually enough.

As I mentioned to Jack a few minutes ago...

- or -

I spoke with Jim and Charlie about this subject, and they...

Find substitutes for "bridge words"

I don't know what else to call these—the "um-ah," the "and-ah," the "y'know," or the "see." I call them bridge words. Most of us occasionally hang these on the ends of sentences, or sometimes in the middle, as we speak. Listeners generally ignore them, but when they occur repeatedly in a lengthy presentation, they begin to grate on the audience.

Getting rid of them is tough. Simply finding out that we pepper our speech with these is usually enough to get us to bite our tongues when a bridge word is ready to fly out. You can find out by recording your presentations on audio or video tape, or by asking a friendly audience such as one in a presentation-skills class to give you an honest appraisal. When people tell us we say "um-ah" a lot, the sting of this criticism works to help us curb the bad habit.

If you can't stop, try substituting something else at the points where you might insert a bridge word. After you've made a point, try "next" or "item" or "first, second, third…"

Recap your message

Restate your case or your proposal when you've finished, preferably showing how the flow of logic brought you to this point.

> *You've seen how these problems developed, and the damage they caused. You've seen the results we were able to obtain with the new systems. And you've seen the economy and productivity that these systems promise for the future. Now, it's time to act to keep them in place.*
>
> - or -
>
> *We have an opportunity, and we have the means to take advantage of it. We have the facilities, the people, the financial resources and most of all the determination. Friends, the time to start is now.*

End it fearlessly

What do you say after *the time to start is now*?

Nothing! Let your last words hang in the air, like the last notes from the choir in a great cathedral. Finish saying what you have to say, look the audience in the eyes and take a step backward.

Don't say *Thank you very much*, and don't ask *Do you have any questions?*

If you believe you did a good job, you should reveal it in your physical presence before the group. Confidence really shows. You should stand there with the posture of one who is fully prepared to answer any questions, but doesn't really believe there will be any.

Thanking the audience is a poor substitute for *I'm finished now, and it's okay to applaud.* And asking for questions acknowledges that you may have done a poor job, or missed something important.

If people have questions, they will ask. Wait for them.

Handling Questions

You finished your presentation forcefully, then took a step back and got a nice round of applause. You're still looking like someone who knows he or she did a good job and who is really prepared for any questions. You are still in charge.

Now, a couple of hands are in the air. What do you do next?

Listen to the question

If that sounds obvious, think about the speakers you've watched nodding while someone poses a question. You can almost hear the speaker thinking, *Here it comes again, the same stupid question I've answered a dozen times.* That is terribly disrespectful, not only of the questioner but of the entire audience.

Worse, this attitude can make you miss the real question, which might be hanging on the end of what this person says. He or she starts by commenting about some subject but ends the question on a quite different topic. You stop listening after the first few words, act bored, and end up delivering a perfectly sound answer to the wrong question.

Repeat the question

There are three reasons for this. First, it's good manners. You are making sure everyone heard the question.

Second, it ensures that you understand the question.

I believe this question relates to the quality issues... No, what I'm getting at is the shipment quantities. Oh, okay, glad to answer that.

Third, and most important, repeating the question gives you a little time to construct an answer.

The gentleman asks about how we plan to deal with the combined problems of material scarcity in the Pacific Northwest and the shortage of skilled labor in our Midwestern facilities.

That can give you almost fifteen seconds. Plenty of time.

Understand the questioner's agenda

People ask questions of speakers for a variety of reasons. Some are genuinely interested in a point you may not have covered. Some ask questions of everybody.

A few ask questions to do backflips in front of the boss. If you know that's going on, chances are everyone else in the room knows it, too. So, don't bounce this questioner; just deal with the question and move on.

And don't argue. You might be stepping on a butterfly without knowing it.

Oh, poor Grace! She never asked about anything before, and that bully is beating her up.

Try to begin your response with agreement, even if you're going to end up someplace else.

I like that approach, and we use it as often as we can. I'd like to have done it that way in this case, had we been able to deal more effectively with the material shortage. Unfortunately, as you know...

Be honest

Sometimes it's hard to admit you don't know the answer, especially if you're the captain. But if you try to bluff your way through an answer, you may find that someone in the audience knows better.

You've estimated something at "around 30 to 33 percent." A hand goes up, and someone says, *The study we've just finished shows the share has been over 50 percent for the past two years.* You look like a fool.

How much better to have used the knowledge of that person in the audience...

The question is about the current percentage, and I must say I don't know, but I'll bet another of our guests has something current on it. Can anyone help us on this point?

Use the answers to reinforce your presentation

Very often, a question will enable you to go back to your presentation and repeat a point. This builds emphasis and memorability.

Yes, we could take a great deal of the cost out of the product by substituting that material. This relates to my comment about safety; you'll remember that I said we will not compromise the safety of anything that will end up in the consumer's hands. So, despite the cost, we have no choice but to stay with our present material.

Handling the sharpshooter

Very rarely, someone will try to twist your tail in the question-and-answer session. Who knows why; maybe he doesn't like your tie. Questions from wise guys, or sharpshooters, seem to have a pattern in the way they begin...

Why should we simply accept that you...

- or -

What is it with you guys and the way you seem to...

- or -

Why do you people always...

- or -

Were you serious when you said...

When a question like this hangs in the air, every eyeball will click your way. The audience doesn't much care about the question; they just want to see how you handle a difficult questioner.

Keep your cool, Boss. Think about the question and repeat the question. And while you do that, *take one step forward*. This is not menacing the questioner, but it's a signal to the audience that you won't retreat from the question.

Then, recognizing that the question probably is about some issue of credibility or trust, use your company's reputation or your own to blockade any further discussion.

> *Yes, I ask you to believe it will work. I'm the person responsible for making sure it does. I am putting everything I have into this project.*
>
> *I won't be satisfied until every customer is satisfied. That's a promise.*
>
> - or -
>
> *It's a sensible question, in light of some problems our industry had historically with the reliability of this equipment. That's why I am proud to rest on my company's record, which has been the benchmark for quality and reliability.*

Have the last word

If you've answered questions after your presentation, it would be wise to do another quick recap. If you do not, the last words the audience remembers might be those of a questioner.

Rephrase and abbreviate your last few lines in order to have the last word.

Using Graphic Aids

A good vocal presentation can be made better through the wise use of visual aids—slides, video or computer-generated images. But be careful; don't let the graphic images become crutches that must be relied on to keep your presentation moving and memorable. An audience soon senses it when a speaker is nervously hiding behind graphics in order to deflect attention from the vocal delivery.

If you feel comfortable with a speech that has no graphics, and you're certain that you can impart any needed imagery with words, have at it. But if there are messages that need illustration, use them with confidence. Just use as few as possible.

I've noticed that in most companies, it's either no graphics in a speech or graphics throughout the speech. Nobody seems to want to use, say, two images if that's all that is called for by the situation. It's easy: if you're using slides, just put dark-colored plain ones ahead, behind and between the few information slides you're using. The audience won't be distracted by a blank screen, but they'll know you have something to show them. With computer-driven images, it's even easier.

"Live" drawings keep it fresh

Flip charts are great for moving information quickly and memorably. They're as fresh as this minute, and the audience will be captivated while you draw or write on them. Sad to say, they're falling out of use as more and more presenters come to believe they'll fail without their laptop-powered images.

Hand-drawn overhead transparencies are fresh, too. The major differences are that they can be seen by a larger audience than flip charts, and they permit the speaker to face the audience while drawing on them. If you find yourself talking to the paper as you write or draw on flip charts, start using overheads instead.

Slides

The use of 35mm slides is called for when you need to show something in great photographic detail. A plant site, a big product, a large-scale work scene such as a construction site...

They have some disadvantages. One is the amount of time required to change them; they're hard to get much quicker than overnight. The other is that slides are the nemesis of the technophobe.

Let's see...I think they go in the projector upside-down, and with the emulsion side toward the screen...or is it the other way?

Yes, that's the right way. Upside down, dull side to the screen. But sometimes you can't tell one side from the other, so be sure to rehearse. If a slide can get into a projector incorrectly, it will.

It's very embarrassing to have the name of the company appear backwards on a building, or to show the chairman at the sales award dinner, pointing at a sign that says SREDAEL SELAS EMOCLEW.

Computer-driven images

PowerPoint, Freelance and Netscape presentations are quick and easy to assemble, and they make it possible to put interesting color, typestyles, illustrations and other attention-grabbing material on the screen. Photographs can be scanned in at the last minute.

If you're handy with a portable computer, you probably already use this method to illustrate your presentations. But if you're not, be sure to bring along the house expert when you present with them. Your audience doesn't want to watch you fumble.

Keep the graphics simple, clear and easy to read. Use very little copy, and don't read it to the audience. Deliver one major idea or point per graphic to keep the show moving. When you wish to show a list of items, keep it to about four per graphic, and "fly" them to the screen one at a time.

Computer-driven images are slick and effective, but don't let them enslave you, the speaker. Remember that the audience has come here to learn something from you, not from the person who made the images. Keep your presentation out front, using the screen images to reinforce, explain, illustrate or otherwise support what you're saying.

The test of your reliance on these and other graphic aids is your ability to perform if the power goes out.

Thomas E. Fuszard

Video

Videotape may be the most effective medium of all. It has crisp images, color, motion, sound, background music, special effects—everything we're used to in entertainment and information television. And most of us know how to push the cassette into the VCR and hit "play."

But most users will do just that—push the button and stand there alongside the audience, watching the video. That takes the speaker out of the scene, and might even make the viewers wonder why he or she is there.

> *I could be watching this thing at home, in my living room…*
> *My eight-year-old could be showing us this video…*
> *Doesn't this guy have anything to say?*

Suggestion: provide the voice-over yourself. Since most corporate videos run just five or six minutes, even on a sophisticated new product, you'd have to watch it no more than two or three times to know roughly what is said as each scene appears. Turn on the video, turn off the sound and let the images remind you of what to say. If there's a clip that has someone talking to the camera, just turn up the sound for that portion.

This keeps you in the presentation, where you belong.

Reminders

Check to see that spare bulbs and other paraphernalia are available. You won't need a spare bulb unless you don't have one.

And, yes, rehearse the hell out of your graphics. You can't overdo it.

Some Details

About You

Try to avoid flashy clothes, ties or any exposed badges, pens or glasses that will detract attention from you. If you're wearing a 15-year service pin, some in the audience will wonder what it means, so you may not have their full attention. Leave it on the dresser.

If you're wearing a dress shirt and tie, I suggest the newest shirt in the closet. Stage fright can give you a tightness in the throat, and an old shirt that may have shrunk a size or two will make this worse.

Be careful about what you eat before presenting. Eat light, avoiding dairy products or heavy sweets that can make you keep clearing your throat. Avoid carbonated beverages, too; that carbonation may return at an inappropriate moment.

Caffeine is not a good idea, even if you're a regular coffee drinker. On top of the adrenaline you're producing, it can make you really jumpy.

The temptation to throw down an alcoholic drink or two can be alluring, especially if you are trying to calm your nerves. Don't do it. The little nervousness you feel will keep you at your best, and booze would only dull you.

Just plain water, no ice.

Thomas E. Fuszard

About your body language

Speakers often ask, "What should I do with my hands?"

Do anything you like <u>except</u> grip the lectern, put a hand in a pocket, or fiddle with toys. If you put a hand into a pocket and absently jingle keys or change, the microphone will pick up the noise and amplify it. And if you continue to play with a pen, pointer or book, the constant distraction will annoy your audience.

Keep your hands free. If you typically make a lot of hand gestures as you speak, fine. That's you.

And please don't write anything on your script having to do with gestures, such as *look right, look left, gesture right...* Your audience will pick up on it right away, and you'll look like a puppet.

About your voice

Speak to the back row. That will make certain you're heard throughout the room. If that makes you a bit loud for the folks in front, not to worry; they'll think you are forceful.

Be sure to do some voice warmups before speaking, especially if you're on early in the morning. You won't want to be clearing your throat or reaching for water when you discover that there's phlegm in your throat.

Americans are afflicted with mumble-itis, which makes everything sounds like "cinnamon rolls."

The airline captain says, *Today, we will be passing over Toledo and cinnamon rolls...*

The subway conductor, *Watch the closing doors; next stop cinnamon rolls.*

The restaurant hostess: *Cinnamon rolls, party of five...*

Try this to improve diction: hold a wooden pencil sideways in your front teeth and say, *These six ships must search sector seven.* Repeat it until you think you're speaking clearly around the handicap of that pencil—eight or ten times. Then take the pencil out and say it again.

You sound clearer, don't you?

Here's another: try these practice lines, which exercise various parts of the vocal mechanism:

Frank's five friends fought furiously.
Betty Barker baked better bread.
Luckily, Larry left the ladders.
Ken cleaned copper kettles.
Glenn guarded gaggles of geese.

The Script

Speech language

If you write your own material for the usual business purposes but shy away from writing your own speeches, fear not! It's really quite simple. Write what you have to say as if you were planning to publish it as an essay, an article or a chapter of a book. Then, come back and do a little tinkering to put it into the pattern or rhythm of a speech.

Remember to enumerate items in the text when you can, and to use short words and short sentences.

To edit the material into speech form, we need to create some of those high points, or sound bites, that we want the audience to carry away.

This can be done in several ways. One is to tinker with grammar in ways that create emphasis and memorability.

Not long ago, a Member of Parliament was heard to say during the weekly *Questions for the Prime Minister, Madam Speaker, it ain't gonna happen that way!* Grammatically incorrect? Yes. Forceful? Also yes.

Without abusing the language, you might translate a comment such as: *We cannot permit this to go on any longer.* changing it to: *Have we had enough? Yes! Are we going to stand for this any longer? No!*

Alliteration is another tool that can be used to draw attention to a line or an idea. Who can forget *nattering nabobs of negativism...*

It's easy to find opportunities to rearrange language to create alliteration. You've written: *They had confidence in the Farnham plan, which flopped miserably.*

And now, you had some fun translating it to: *I am one who bears scars for his faith in the project now known as Farnham's famous folly!*

Be careful not to overdo it with alliteration. If it's forced and frequent, your audience may gag on it.

The use of parallelisms is another way to create memorability. Remember this? *If a free society cannot help the many who are poor, it cannot save the few who are rich.*

And how about, *Where peace is unknown, make it welcome; where peace is fragile, make it strong; where peace is temporary, make it permanent.*

Or, *...crimes so heinous, we cannot tolerate their being ignored because we cannot survive their being repeated.*

It takes very little time to scan your written work and find opportunities to draw parallelisms.

You have written: *Government may find that in some areas these are plentiful and in others quite scarce. Some Washington leaders can see in this nothing but opportunities for revenue enhancement, rather than volume growth.*

You make this into: *To some people in government, these issues of abundance and scarcity mean more taxes and less growth.*

Keep looking at your material, and chances are you'll find a chance to build yet another memory "spike" —a tripartite construction. These are very memorable.

Lincoln: *We cannot dedicate, we cannot consecrate, we cannot hallow this ground.*

Roosevelt: *I see one-third of a nation ill-housed, ill-clad, ill-nourished.*

In your material, you find: *There can be a lot of satisfaction in managing one's own business. The feeling of involvement is great, and the opportunity to watch something grow is hard to duplicate. Even the risk of* portunity to watch something grow is hard to duplicate. Even the risk of failure brings a measure of exhilaration.

There's a tripartite construction inside, waiting to be free:

> *In managing one's own business, there can be no higher satisfaction than the feeling of involvement; no stronger motivation than the risk of failure; no greater enjoyment than watching it grow.*

Same material, more memorably stated.

The format

Give your eyes a break. Put your script into type large enough so you can leave your granny glasses in your pocket. The use of 18-point Helvetica or Arial should do it. Use wide margins and generous spacing, and don't have anything printed on the bottom third of the page.

The normal format in which we read printed material is the format of this paragraph. To read it, your eyes must follow a serpentine course, crossing each line from left to right and then returning for the next line, just like a typewriter or the cursor on your computer. That's fine for the written word, but it requires a lot of attention, which means that your eyes spend more time on the page than on the audience. Reading the speech without looking at the people sitting there can be really annoying to them. They may be wondering why they're not simply reading this stuff in their own offices, or perhaps in the comfort of their living rooms.

Word From the Top
The Chief Executive's Guide to Business Communication

My system for helping speakers pick up language from the script more easily might work for you. It breaks the language into phrases or small groups of words that can be captured visually without really "reading" in the standard left-to-right way. This permits you to glance down, pick up a line and then deliver it while looking at the audience.

Here is a sample, first using a standard page layout:

Fourscore and seven years ago our fathers brought forth on this continent, a new nation, conceived in Liberty, and dedicated to the proposition that all men are created equal.

Now we are engaged in a great civil war, testing whether that nation or any nation so conceived and so dedicated can long endure. We are met on a great battlefield of that war. We have come to dedicate a portion of that field, as a final resting place for those who here gave their lives that that nation might live. It is altogether fitting and proper that we should do this.

Now, see it in a phrased format:

Fourscore and seven years ago
    our fathers brought forth,
    on this continent,
    a new nation—

Thomas E. Fuszard

>> conceived in Liberty,
>> and dedicated to the proposition
>> that all men are created equal.
> Now we are engaged
>> in a great civil war,
>> testing whether that nation,
>> or any nation
>> so conceived and so dedicated,
>> can long endure.
> We are met
>> on a great battlefield
>> of that war.
> We have come to dedicate
>> a portion of that field
>> as a final resting place
>> for those who here gave their lives
>> that that nation might live.
> It is altogether fitting and proper
>> that we should do this.

Try reading both of these aloud. Then, try both of them aloud in front of a mirror. You will see much more of yourself in the mirror with the phrased method. The punctuation is changed only slightly to assist with pacing, and indents are there to show you when you might get a breath.

This system requires <u>no training</u> and <u>no practice</u>. Just substitute it for the regular page layout you're using in speech scripts. You will find it easy to use even in a cold reading and very comfortable after you've rehearsed once or twice. As you become more familiar with the content, you'll probably reach down and grasp more than one line at a time, making you sound even more relaxed and confident.

As a final editing step, reduce as many long and complex words as possible into simpler language. If you want to be heard and understood by those in the back row, make those short, Anglo-Saxon words your friends. Short words are simple to mouth and unmistakable to hear. This is *not* "dumbing-down" a speech; it's improving communication by making it easier for both you and the listener.

If you are discussing *the U.S. automotive industry*, for example, you will be understood perfectly if during your speech you shift to *the auto industry* or *the car business*. They're easier to say, too.

Making it ring

For most kinds of oral and written business communication, ordinary language does the job just fine. But the language of a speech to 1,200 conventioneers is not the language of an across-the-table luncheon conversation.

If you want your remarks to ring from the rafters, you must tune your ear to the great voices around us. And if you cannot spare the time to read the works of great speakers in printed form, at least take a moment to check C-Span from time to time to see what's going on. You'll find some good material and some excellent deliveries.

When your ear is tuned to "speechmaking language," you may begin to convert some of your work into more memorable messages.

You might have said this across a lunch table:

I think that as one of the few superpowers in the world, this country has a special responsibility for leadership.

But this message is delivered in your keynote address as:

America must rise to shoulder the great burden that history thrusts upon great nations.

You may have told an associate:

Customer service is really important, and if we don't do a good job there, all the rest of what we do doesn't really matter.

But in front of the entire workforce you might say:

This is critical, for if we fail in customer service, we fail everywhere.

Word From the Top
The Chief Executive's Guide to Business Communication

Thomas E. Fuszard

The Word in Meetings

Introduction

Much of the information that fuels American business is exchanged in meetings. Indeed, many business leaders would feel paralyzed if this medium of information exchange disappeared. Some already complain that the new distributed-workforce systems do not provide enough opportunity for live interaction between employees.

Nevertheless, attendance at meetings leads the list when employees are asked which of their activities wastes the most time.

> *We have far too many meetings.*
> *Our meetings last too long.*
> *I never see my boss; she's always in a meeting.*
> *Nobody listens to me in meetings; there's no participation.*
> *The boss is just showing his authority.*
> *I've heard all that before.*
> *We go over the same stuff we received on paper.*
> *These things turn into lectures or sermons.*
> *We have no agenda, and nobody would follow it anyway.*
> *People are always trying to grab the spotlight.*
> *Meetings are a giant waste of time.*

I have no time any more; I'm always in meetings.

People around here think meetings are our only business.

Time Management

The study of meetings is as much about time management as about information exchange. So, let's start by thinking about time. If you're like most chief executives, you often think:

There doesn't seem to be enough time in the day.
I can't seem to finish anything.
I have this uneasy feeling about my own use of time.
My people are wasting far too much time.
I'm working too many hours, too many days.

Common complaints, all of them. Everybody is looking for some way to find more time, or to get more out of the time we spend on the job. The feeling grows more intense as workforces shrink, leaving more to be done by fewer people.

The arithmetic of time management is quite simple. Your people probably work an eight-hour day, a 40-hour week. This usually works out to 240 days a year, net of weekends, holidays and normal vacations. And since we have 240 work days a year and each comprises 480 minutes, even my poor math tells me that anything that occupies two minutes a day is equal to one day a year.

So, if you come into the office and spend five minutes each morning chatting with the folks around the coffee machine, you've occupied two and a half of your 240 days coming up to speed on football scores, hearing about great fishing trips and looking at pictures of somebody's kids.

Is this a good use of your time? Yes, probably, but only you can judge that.

Let's say you often walk down to the big copier to make a copy of a single letter, and two or three times a week find that the machine is in use on a big print run. This requires that you return to make a copy. Two or three times a week, two minutes each way...that's a whole day. You've spent the equivalent of a whole day's time on what? Making copies? No, *just finding out that you can't.* You have to come back and spend another day to actually print them.

Now, take this simple arithmetic into the meeting room. If your Monday morning staff meeting lasts just an hour, it's taken *six days* from the 240-day work year of everyone present. If it lasts all morning, as some do, this meeting has occupied *five weeks* of the life of every participant.

Again, the question: Is this a good use of everyone's time? Perhaps, but *you* must answer that. Only you can change the frequency of meetings, the duration of meetings and, most important, the content of meetings.

If you are truly concerned about time management, meetings are a good place to start.

Planning the Meeting

The best time to save time in a meeting is before it starts. Think about the various reasons to have a meeting:

> *To find agreement*
> *To explain something*
> *To report on an activity, a plan, a trip*
> *To demonstrate a product*
> *Because it's Tuesday at 8:30*

No, that last one doesn't make much sense, does it? Most regularly scheduled meetings will be pointless at least some of the time. This is one reason it's a good idea to have one-subject meetings. Another is that regular meetings tend to grow as people are "promoted" to attendance.

> *I now sit in the company's regular executive review meetings.*
>
> - or -
>
> *I'm in there with all the top people every Friday.*

Be fearless about the need for meetings. Are you being asked to referee a disagreement between people or departments? Could a meeting between two people do what's needed? Is somebody just trying to do backflips for the boss?

Question people hard about why, or if, the meeting they want makes sense. You'll find that you won't have to question the motives very often. Your staff will get the idea.

Question yourself, too. As you're getting dressed tomorrow morning, ask *Am I calling today's meeting just because I have the rank?*

Remember that everybody knows you wear the stripes; you don't have to prove it.

More questions: When should you be involved? Why is the chief executive required to know about this material? Will participants be reluctant to speak their minds with the boss present?

And, finally: Would some other method of communication work as well? There's a long list of choices, from e-mail to letters to memos to phonemail to newsletters. Remember that these other methods reach everyone, whereas the meeting reaches only those who aren't traveling, or out sick, or on vacation. What's more, a written summary can be studied, copied, circulated, taken home…and the meeting cannot.

Oddly, some businesspeople say, *We send copies of everything to the people who weren't there,* perhaps without having thought of doing that in the first place.

By the way, if you're a bear about creating more paperwork, remember that adding a piece of paper to the stack on someone's desk is a lot better than taking two hours of his or her time for a meeting.

Who's invited?

Check this list to see who should be invited to your meeting:

> *All members of the department*
> *Everybody who is available*
> *Everybody who was here last time*
> *Everybody who's interested*
> *Everybody who needs to know, to contribute, to act*

Only the last group makes sense *all the time*. If you must have regular meetings, be careful about those participants who are being asked to participate just once, and who may then feel they've been promoted to attendance. Make it clear that this is a one-time event. For the same reason, don't announce the next meeting at this one; nobody will be out of joint about not being invited.

It's wise to keep paring the attendance lists, too. Remember that we're trying to save time, and if you can cut two or three names from a two-hour weekly meeting, you are giving back to the company two or three hundred hours of high-cost time.

Do you really feel that people's egos may be bruised by being disinvited? You probably will be surprised...

Carl, I've noticed that almost none of the material in the XYZ meeting relates to your activity, and I have the impression that you'd much rather be here in your department than in that meeting room. Would you prefer to be cut loose from that weekly gathering?

The agenda

Who planned this meeting, and why? Did anyone else contribute discussion topics, or is it a one-subject meeting? Is it planned for a manageable amount of time, or is that unclear? Does everyone on the list need to hear all of it, or should we plan two meetings? How about a meeting in which everyone hears one part, and half the group leaves during the other part? Does this agenda suggest a reasonable outcome or goal?

Who's in charge?

Meetings tend to be run by the highest-ranking participant, rather than by a project leader or another person who may be the most knowledgeable about the subject. Keep your feet out of this trap by designating *in advance* one of the experts as chairperson for each meeting, as his or her leadership is appropriate to the topic.

If the meeting is to cover a number of topics, or if it's a regularly scheduled review meeting, try rotating the leadership among the participants. You may not have a better way to see how up-and-coming people handle themselves under a little stress—how they deal with new ideas, difficult people, conflict. Take off your stripes and attend as an ordinary participant. You'll still be there to intervene if things get out of hand.

Preparation reminders

You want your people to be at their best, so be careful about meeting dates and times. On Fridays, many brains have already quit for the week, and on Mondays they may still be scrambled from doing heaven-knows-what on the weekend. Likewise the days before and after holidays.

Meetings should be on neutral turf, not in someone's cave. And although food service is neighborly, it's not necessary.

The meeting notice or invitation should indicate date, time, place, agenda, presenters, leadership and attendees. That should be enough to help invitees decide between this meeting and some other urgent business.

Make sure everything that's needed for the meeting is ordered or reserved, and test-run any equipment you will be using. The second-leading reason meetings fail (the first is inadequate or unused agendas) is the lack of materials and equipment.

Conducting the meeting

Watch the clock. Beginning punctually sends an important message about your meeting leadership. Announce the schedule and the agenda, then repeat the expectations.

We've scheduled this meeting to last no more than one hour. We will review the vendor recommendations, and we aim to make a final selection.

Be sure to mention any agenda-item cancellations, so those present only for those items can leave. Try to organize the other topics so that matters of general interest are first and, at a break, allow those who have no interest in the remaining topics to leave.

Stick with the agenda. If one person tries to go into an unrelated area, remember that everyone else is counting on you to keep things moving...

Time permitting, we'll take that up at the end of this meeting, or perhaps schedule another meeting to discuss it separately.

Deal with questions about each agenda item before moving on to the next. A general question-and-answer session at the end, dealing with all agenda items, can become a free-for-all. Worse, some people may have left when their segment of the agenda was completed, so they won't be around for questions.

Disagreements may arise; scrapping should not. If a couple of people get into it, act right away.

Fred, Jim, we'll need to park that item for now and get on with the agenda. I'd like you to come to some agreement before we take up this matter again.

If someone has an important question, it will surface in the discussion of that topic. *Do not* make a general solicitation of questions on all topics. That's because someone may be harboring a question that is of interest to him or her alone, and will be reluctant to ask in a group, but that question will spill out if you open the door this way...

Let's go around the table one last time, starting with you, Stuart. Anything on your mind?

Every attendee will cringe, hoping Stuart will be silent. Everyone will want to choke him, and you, if he opens his mouth.

You can discourage these backflips-for-the-boss questions by doing an occasional walkabout in the office. That gives the staff at least a moment's "face time" with the chief and may make them feel it's unnecessary to try to captivate you with a clever question during a meeting.

After discussion and questions, recap the meeting quickly before you adjourn to let everyone know what you think you accomplished and what needs to be done.

Thanks, everyone, for your participation. We've agreed on the next steps for the XYZ program, and each of the committees has its assignment. We know what the costs will be. We've specified the equipment, and we are ready to put this work out for bids. We're adjourned.

Don't give up

Some managers think it takes too much time and trouble to review all these aspects of meeting agendas, invitations lists and the rest. Some may think that doing so might create friction. So, they go with the flow and just keep on attending all those meetings. And the meetings get longer, and less purposeful.

But adding some discipline to the planning and conduct of your company's meetings will yield big returns in time and effectiveness. It's important. So, stay with it.

Thomas E. Fuszard

The Heard Word

Dictionary definitions of "communicate" use words such as *impart knowledge...make known...give to another...interchange thoughts...*all of which involve both sending messages and receiving them. Everything else in this book deals with sending; this is about the other part—the difficult part for most of us.

Americans don't listen well. We tune out as soon as we determine that what we're hearing is too old, too boring, too complicated. We allow today's information flood to wash over our consciousness without really paying attention to much of it. We move from a room where someone on television is explaining another view of a Cabinet member walking to his car, and into a room where a mind-numbing radio talk show is shifting from the banal to the inane on the quarter-hour.

We're being trained to understand that we don't really have to listen. Television makes sure we never miss anything by repeating endlessly the day's news clips or sports action.

Here's a different view of back-to-school day, with a closeup of the weary teachers. Now, for a bigger picture, let's go to Bill in Chopper One...

- or -

This reverse-angle view of the play shows clearly that the quarterback's foot was over the line at the time the ball was released...

- or -

Let's replay that action as the police close in...

- or -

Here you see how that ball took an extra hop in front of his glove...

Knowing that everything will be repeated makes us lazy. Just think about how much more attentive you are at a football or baseball game than you are while watching a game on television.

Maybe the intellectual filters we've developed are really useful. They do keep our brains from being gridlocked with meaningless verbal trash. But they don't seem to discriminate in favor of the useful information we need, so some of us miss it.

Does it matter?

Some might feel that because they've reached the top, others are now paid to listen to them, not the other way around. That's backwards. The best chief executives are the best listeners—the people with endless curiosity about how things work, eagerness to scoop up information, willingness to wait for an answer and genuine respect for others' contributions.

We learn nothing while talking.

Good listening saves time and money. It avoids misunderstandings, prevents mistakes and removes the need for re-works. It saves the time required for repairs and exchanges. It lowers warranty expense and the cost of refunds.

Somebody figured out that if every American worker made only one ten-dollar mistake a year, the cost would amount to a billion dollars.

You didn't pay close attention to the invitation, so you've arrived at the meeting site two and a half hours early.

You thought the numbers you heard were before depreciation, not after, so the information you gave analysts was wrong.

Jack James is in Cleveland and Jim Jackson is on his way to Cincinnati, both the wrong places, based on your instructions.

The sales rep warned long ago that the machine you just installed couldn't handle this volume. You thought he meant the other one.

Good listening demonstrates politeness. Think about the people you like to talk to, and those you don't, and ask yourself which of them tend to listen well. Good listeners are generally more likeable. Most of us think they're more intelligent, too.

Test your listening habits.

Not everybody who made it to the chief exec's job got there because he or she was a good listener:

- *Do you routinely prepare your next comment while someone is speaking to you?*
- *Have you found that your mind wandered during a conversation, so you didn't know what someone just said?*

- *Have you ever been caught looking at your watch?*
- *Do you ignore people with accents, or those who speak slowly?*
- *Do you ever interrupt others?*
- *Does your vision ever wander from the person who's speaking?*
- *Do you like to have the last word in a conversation?*
- *Do people often correct your misunderstandings?*

It's easy to flunk. Just one or two *yes* answers means you're probably not a good listener.

You have plenty of company, much as the rest of us don't like to admit it. We like to think we are quick-witted, and find comfort in our belief that speedy intelligence always is accompanied by impatience. We like to hear speech at the rate of 180 words per minute or so, not the 120- to 150-word rate at which most people speak. When our minds wander from a slow or dry speaker, it's because we're bright, right?

It's odd that with all the training we get in reading—the visual means of acquiring knowledge—we receive little or no training in how to listen, even though that is the way we gather a great deal of what we know.

Only in the military are we directed to pay attention:

Listen up, you people!
All right, gimme your attention!
Now hear this...

Thomas E. Fuszard

At ease!

And only in the military are the sanctions for not listening swift and severe.

Hearing and listening

The difference between hearing and listening is the difference between *passive listening* and *active listening*.

Passive listening is the kind we practice when we do something other than take notes while we talk on the telephone, or when we work while the radio or television is playing. It's demonstrated when we work while those around us are conversing. Our hearing is still turned on, but our brains are running at idle.

Active listening begins when something drags us into the conversation or brings our attention to the broadcast.

What did you think about that, Tom?

Hey, look at the great gift Annie brought us!

We interrupt this broadcast...

Now, for breaking news about the quake, let's go to our anchor desk in New York.

Perhaps the attention-getter is something as simple as hearing your doctor say, *Uh-oh.*

Now, the hearing is tuned precisely, the eyes turn to the source, the brain shifts out of neutral. We're alert, ready to suck up information.

Some suggestions

This is about active listening. It's about ways to engage ourselves in the communication process, and to stay engaged...

Be a good audience

Make it clear that you welcome the conversation or presentation. Establish that you want to help the speaker present his or her message.

> *Sure, I have plenty of time. Let's sit down over here.*
>
> - or -
>
> *Discuss the XYZ plan? I'd love to; just give me a minute to finish this memo.*
>
> - or -
>
> *Let me switch the phone so we're not interrupted.*

This is more than simple politeness. It's a way to make sure you get the most from the speaker, and it helps ensure you won't be distracted from the message.

Put aside biases.

We all have them, and you'll do well to understand that. Perhaps you have trouble focusing on comments made in a heavy accent. Maybe there's a cultural bias underlying your feelings when you hear a name that seems obviously Italian, or Polish, or Vietnamese. Or, maybe the person speaks very slowly. It could be that you don't take young people seriously because they have little experience. (Guilty: I often calculate that I've been in the business community longer than some clients have been alive. I have pants older than most of them.)

Perhaps something about this speaker's manner annoys you. You might think she is crude, or pushy, or slick, or arrogant or maybe just a little too clever. You distrust her. You tune out.

We pre-judge all the time. Sometimes we'll select a product because the salesperson seemed warm and sincere, then learn that a better product was offered by the person we thought was too aggressive or promotional.

Even a person's apparel can affect our feelings about what they have to say. Show up at a luxury automobile dealership in black leather on a motorcycle, as I have, and you'll see what I mean.

Is this the right time?

Timing is essential to effective communication. If the time isn't right for you or for the other participant, your attempt to hear and understand a message clearly may flop.

I need to get back to the project. I wonder how long this will take.

- or -

He just lost his brother, so I know that must be on his mind.

- or -

Wow, this guy seems really angry!

When in doubt, speak up.

> *Is this a good time for you to discuss it?*
>
> - or -
>
> *I have a great deal on my mind today. Could we reschedule?*
>
> - or -
>
> *I have a feeling another time would be better for this.*

Be alert to messages and motives.

It's important to try to get behind a speaker's comments to find the emotional sparkplugs that may be firing this communication. The process may be polluted by anger, fear, suspicion, distrust...who knows what.

A friend says he's lost interest in his power boat...

I'd better be careful what I say; maybe he can't afford it any longer.

A worker says he's being picked on, singled out by his boss...

He could be saying he's done a bad job, and got caught. Maybe he's over his head and looking for help.

A fellow worker says he's bored...

Maybe he doesn't have enough to do; what else could we give him that's within his scope?

A man says that only women and minorities get promoted...

Is he feeling threatened about his own limited abilities?

Some of this can be difficult to sort out—the love, hate, fear, jealousy, frustration, worry, rage. Try to understand the speaker's worst fears and greatest hopes; it's a place to start.

Get your body to behave.

We may think we're listening, but our bodies give us away. If you say you're not concerned, but clench your fists or drum your fingers, your body is broadcasting signals. If you say you're excited about a program, but slouch, yawn and gaze away while you say it, you're not likely to be believed. If the speaker notices that you have your arms folded, or if you're fiddling with your keys, communication will deteriorate.

Try to get your physical actions and posture in synch with the conversation. React to the speaker with a nod, a headshake, a smile—any signal that you are attentive and that you understand.

Try silence.

Most of us are so in love with the sound of our own voices, it seems we can't hear them enough. We tell ourselves we are good listeners, but we seldom shut up long enough to prove it.

Holding your tongue is a great way to get more information and better information from a speaker. When he or she finishes a comment, give a nod or some indication that you understand, but say nothing. After a moment, the speaker will enrich the conversation with all kinds of additional information and perhaps more true feelings about the subject.

Don't be afraid of a pause. The speaker *will* say more.

Think about the outline or summary you'll prepare

This can be the best single way of improving your listening skills. Build a little anxiety into your listening experience by imagining that you will be responsible for recalling and writing what was said. It will require that you pay close attention and that you retain the high points from what you've heard.

Take notes

Notetaking honors the speaker's comments and proves you're paying attention. It aids your own memorization. Perhaps best, it can keep you focused on the speaker and away from the preparation of your next comment.

This can be scary for people talking to the boss, but it's extremely effective. It will cause the speaker to think before speaking, and you can bet it will shorten your meetings. Some recommend keeping the notetaking out of sight; I say visible note-taking urges the speaker to be brief, precise and thoughtful.

Longtime communicator and corporate-wars veteran Dave Schaefer says he worked for someone who took notes on little cards. "My response," he says, "was to come in organized and be brief because I never knew where those cards went, and I knew they couldn't hold much information. I've used this technique since I started my own business, knowing it sends the same message to clients who tend to ramble off on other matters."

Thomas E. Fuszard

Learn to ask; ask to learn

First-year journalism students are taught a rhyming memory prompt, drawn from one of Kipling's works, that is designed to stay with them career-long:

> I keep six honest serving men
> *(They taught me all I knew);*
> *Their names are What and Why and When*
> *And How and Where and Who.*

Put the six honest serving men to work for you by using questions to open a dialogue. Questions help ease the other person into his or her comfort zone, dealing with familiar subjects and accurate knowledge.

Open-ended questions are best. They're the kind that cannot be answered with an easy yes or no:

> *What did you do next?*
> *How does that work?*
> *Why is it done that way?*
> *When is it necessary to make a change?*
> *Where is the best place to put the facility?*

Play back what you've learned

Repeat what you've heard. Rephrase it, summarize it, even sketch it. This confirms for the speaker that you fully understand, and it helps etch the information into your memory. It proves that you care enough to have listened attentively.

# # #

Thomas E. Fuszard

The Last Word

Nobody said it would be easy. Now, in a rare leisure moment, you may long for those times back in the plant or the engineering office or the marketing department where life seemed so much simpler. Everybody's picking at you for some message about plans, results, outlook…what about those new products…how's the bank-line negotiation coming along…when can you speak to the investment bankers…and all the rest.

Ever since the Board put you in that chair, and perhaps for some time before that, you've felt that your company is at the center of the universe, with the rest of industry and commerce spinning around it. Nothing wrong with that. It's what you're paid to feel, whether your company is one of the hot-ticket outfits on every stockbrokers's tongue or a grind-it-out smokestack stalwart that nobody seems to know.

It doesn't matter, really. You're the one they are counting on—the Wall Street analyst, the rep in the field, the guy on the third shift in the shop, the many employee families in their homes. You're the voice of the company.

So, keep it short and simple and honest. Write the truth. Edit it to take out the repetition, the junk jargon, the passive voice. Peel it down to the essentials and polish it until it's your best. Rehearse it until it's as familiar as the names of your kids. Then, suck up your gut and get out there and deliver it.

Lots of people are pulling for you. Lots of people want you to win. Break a leg, Boss.

#

About the author

Thomas E. Fuszard is a corporate communications consultant and writer living in Southern California. He has been involved in corporate communications for 40 years. A consultant who provides speechwriting and other editorial services, Fuszard also leads training workshops and coaches executives in business writing and presentation skills.

Tom Fuszard started his career as a reporter for Dun & Bradstreet, Inc. Before establishing his corporate communications practice in 1980, he spent 20 years with three Big Board-listed companies, primarily in investor relations.

#

Printed in the United States
4137